ZEPPELIN OVER SUFFOLK

Against the first light of dawn she was visible, drifting in a disabled condition. She kept turning – her rudders and elevators were probably damaged – and as she came over Theberton, people on the ground could hear the sound of tapping as the crew tried frantically to carry out temporary repairs.

Christopher Elliott, 'The End of Zeppelin L48',
East Anglian Magazine, September 1951.

Perhaps three minutes – perhaps five minutes – is the duration of the airship's death-dive. When she was about 1,000 metres off the ground, I thought I saw one or two comrades – little black specks in the sky – jump out of the blazing torch. Better to be broken to pieces than burnt to death.

Commander Martin Dietrich, quoted in Rolf
Marben, *Zeppelin Adventures* (1931).

As British air defences stiffened, so the terrible vision of Zeppelins falling like blazing comets through the night sky over England was repeated time and time again.

Douglas Botting, *Dr Eckener's Dream Machine* (2001).

Who art thou that judgest another man's servant? To his own master he standeth or falleth.

Inscription on a plaque dedicated to the crew
of Zeppelin L48, taken from the Bible, *Romans* 14:4.

ZEPPELIN OVER SUFFOLK

THE FINAL RAID OF THE L48

MARK MOWER

Pen & Sword
AVIATION

First published in Great Britain in 2008 by
Pen & Sword Military
an imprint of
Pen & Sword Books Ltd
47 Church Street
Barnsley
South Yorkshire
S70 2AS

ISBN 978 1 84415 737 2

A CIP catalogue record for this book is available from the British Library.

Typeset in 11/13pt Plantin by
Mac Style, Beverley, East Yorkshire

Printed and bound in the UK by
Biddles

Pen & Sword Books Ltd incorporates the Imprints of Pen & Sword
Aviation, Pen & Sword Maritime, Pen & Sword Military, Wharncliffe Local
History, Pen & Sword Select, Pen & Sword Military Classics and
Leo Cooper.

For a complete list of Pen & Sword titles please contact
PEN & SWORD BOOKS LIMITED
47 Church Street, Barnsley, South Yorkshire, S70 2AS, England
E-mail: enquiries@pen-and-sword.co.uk
Website: www.pen-and-sword.co.uk

Contents

Dedication

For my wife Jacqueline, daughter Rosie, and favourite cat Monty. An inspiring trio.

Introduction

From the first recorded manned flight in a balloon on 15 October 1783, the history of lighter-than-air craft has been both fascinating and colourful. In ascending above the skyline of Paris in a tethered hot air balloon, the Frenchman Jean-François Pilâtre de Rozier became the first of many intrepid explorers of the sky. Like many others, his enthusiasm for this form of travel rapidly overcame any fears he may have possessed for the fragility of gas-powered flight. Only one month after his first ascent he took to the air again – this time in an untethered balloon, rising to a height of some 3,000ft and travelling for 26 minutes over a distance of more than 7 miles above a jubilant Parisian audience.

The success of this Montgolfier-built craft inspired others to experiment with hydrogen-filled balloons and a number of spectacular flights were attempted, including the crossing of the English Channel on 7 January 1785 by aeronauts Jean-Pierre Blanchard and Dr John Jeffries. Setting off from Dover with a slight north-north-westerly breeze, the pair took just two hours to cross the Channel, being brought to a stop by a tree outside Calais. Competing with them to be the first to achieve this feat was the ever-fearless Pilâtre de Rozier. He prepared a balloon for the flight in the autumn of 1784 but was unable to launch it until after the Blanchard crossing. After several attempts, de Rozier finally set off from Boulogne-sur-Mer on 15 June 1785, accompanied by his friend Pierre Romain. Despite a promising start, the balloon deflated over land and was brought down near Wimereux in the Pas-de-Calais, killing both men. In another first for the French, they became the earliest known victims of an air crash.

Balloons would dominate the next hundred years of aviation history and the military potential of these pioneering craft was

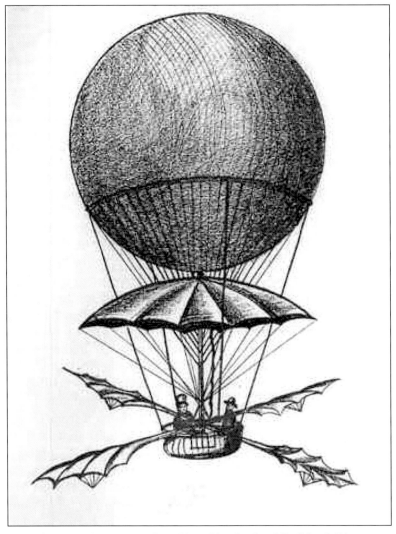

The balloon used by aeronauts Jean-Pierre Blanchard and Dr John Jeffries to cross the English Channel on 7 January 1785.

soon realised. Observation balloons were first used during the Napoleonic era and the earliest balloon corps of *aérostiers* was established on 29 March 1794 under the guidance of scientist Charles Coutelle. The French triumphed over the Austrians at the Battle of Fleurus some three months later, with Coutelle

Charles Coutelle's ascent in an observation balloon during the Battle of Fleurus in June 1794 became the first recorded use of an aircraft for military purposes.

and General Morlot spending the whole of the 10-hour engagement aloft in their tethered balloon, sending orders and observation reports down one of two mooring cables to a ground crew below. The victory of the French was due in no small part to the importance of this ground-breaking aerial reconnaissance.

Both the Union and Confederate armies used balloons for reconnaissance during the American Civil War, the Union army being the first to use aircraft carriers to launch observation balloons, in 1861. News of these developments travelled and in 1863 a young engineering officer in the Prussian Army was sent to the United States to work as a military observer for the Union army and to learn about aerial warfare. He made his first balloon flight in St Paul, Minnesota, and later returned to Germany convinced of the military potential of using gas-powered aircraft. His name was Count Ferdinand Adolf August Heinrich Graf von Zeppelin, and he would later become the inventor of the rigid airship.

The powered flight of the dirigible *La France* on 9 August 1884 demonstrated that there was clear scope to overcome some of the limitations of balloon flight. The airship was powered by an electric motor and airscrew, and could be steered rather than relying on the prevailing direction of the wind. Beyond this, there was rapid progress in developing operational airships in both France and Germany, although it would be the latter that would do most to take airship advancement into the technology-obsessed twentieth century.

The development of the first petrol-driven, high-speed, internal combustion engine, by mechanical engineer and inventor Gottlieb Daimler, took Count Zeppelin's plans for a rigid airship from the drawing board to the factory floor. The advantages of the electric motor used by the airship *La France* were offset by the immense weight of its supporting batteries, making sustained flight unrealistic. With the considerable power-to-weight ratio of the Daimler engine, German airship designers like Count Zeppelin could at last realise their dreams of producing larger and potentially more useful flying machines.

In 1896 Count Zeppelin received the blessing of the prestigious Union of German Engineers for his plans to produce the first rigid airship. Having raised sufficient funds for the project, he began construction of the airship in June 1898 in a floating shed on Lake Constance near Friedrichshafen. The airship took to the air for the first time on the evening of 2 July 1900 in a less than impressive maiden flight, which demonstrated its slowness, the weakness of its hull and the difficulties of steering such a large dirigible – in all other respects this flight was a significant milestone in the history of airship travel.

Count Zeppelin's name would become synonymous with the emergence of giant airships in the period from 1900 to 1940. And of the 161 rigid airships built and flown by Germany in that period, 119 were constructed by the company he founded. His dream was to produce commercial airships that would provide the very best in passenger travel and demonstrate Germany's cutting-edge credentials in technological innovation. But on the eve of the First World War, it was on the military potential of his ships of the sky that the Count concentrated.

When German airships began to attack England in the early part of 1915, Count Zeppelin was regarded as a national hero. Many people, within Germany and beyond, believed that the ability of these aircraft to bring the reality of war to the British home front would prove to be a decisive factor in ending the conflict in Europe. That history was to prove otherwise owed much to another piece of emerging aviation technology – the fixed-wing aircraft.

When the airship L48 emerged from Count Zeppelin's factory facility at Friedrichshafen in May 1917, it was prized by the German Navy for its ability to fly at high altitude, beyond the upper limits of the British ground defences and fledgling home defence squadrons. For those hoping that Zeppelins could yet prove their worth and dominate the night skies above Britain, this airship was the realisation of a long-held faith and a potent weapon of war.

This book tells the remarkable story of the L48. It is a tale of courage, dedication and survival in the midst of a world turned upside down: a world in which men chose to take to the skies in airships without the security of the newly developed pack-parachute and a world in which local people became unwilling participants in a global conflict that did not differentiate between combatants and non-combatants. But it is also a tale about benevolence and the compassion shown by men and women even in the gloomiest days of war, heralding a new dawn after much darkness.

CHAPTER ONE

Prologue – The Quest for Safer Air Travel

The airship rose like a leviathan above the expectant personnel on the Dresden aerodrome. It was a warm summer Sunday in 1914 and the Zeppelin *Sachsen* had climbed to hover at a height of around 4,000ft above the assembled crowd of onlookers. At the controls of the airship was Ernst Lehmann, a young naval engineer who had joined the staff of the German Airship Transportation Company, the operating branch of Count Ferdinand von Zeppelin's DELAG organisation, in 1913. Even at this early stage of aerostat development, the name Zeppelin had become synonymous with German airship advancement and during the next two decades his company would vastly overshadow its rivals in the design and production of over a hundred military and commercial lighter-than-air craft.

Sachsen had been built in 1913 and represented the cutting edge of Zeppelin technology at that time. In addition to an impressive overall length of 470ft, it held within its rigid metal structure numerous gas cells containing just over 700,000ft^3 of inflammable hydrogen gas enabling it to lift around 18,000lb of weight. Two gondolas were slung below its underbelly, a front control car that included an engine room and all of the controls necessary to facilitate the lift, speed, direction and communications of the aircraft, and a separate, rear car housing only an engine. Both gondolas were connected by a walkway, attached to the body of the dirigible like the keel of a ship. The top speed of the airship was a respectable 45mph.

Lehmann had been born in Ludwigshafen in 1886 and was educated at the University of Berlin before joining the navy for military service in 1905. He had spent weeks operating the airship on regular experimental flights for the company between Leipzig and the capital of Saxony. But this was different, for

A brochure advertising the Zeppelin Company's passenger air service.

The Zeppelin airship Sachsen *in 1914.*

today the craft was playing host to a group of inventors intent on demonstrating their latest innovations in the quest for safer air travel. Lehmann was intrigued and somewhat bewildered by the exercise but was pleased to have a distraction from his normal flight routine. Having previously worked in the imperial shipyards at Kiel, and still being in the Naval Reserve, he had joined the Zeppelin organisation searching for excitement. In the previous sixteen months he had piloted commercial airships across Germany on hundreds of flights and had gained plenty of experience in the process. On this particular Sunday in 1914, only weeks before war would be declared, he could not have imagined how much more excitement he would experience in four years as a naval airship captain. Beyond that he would also become a world-famous civilian airship captain, and would eventually meet his end aboard the most infamous airship in history, the *Hindenburg*.

One of the inventors in the control car stepped towards Lehmann clutching a package that looked similar to a large, closed umbrella. He explained that it was the latest design in parachutes and urged the airship captain to try it out. Lehmann was somewhat startled by the request. 'No, thank you', he replied, 'surely you have enough confidence in it. Try it yourself!'

Ernst Lehmann, the well-known Zeppelin airship commander, who flew commercial flights for the company before and after the First World War in addition to his military service.

To the hilarity of the others, the self-conscious inventor declined Lehmann's repeated invitations to step outside the airship and try out the parachute. 'Very well,' said Lehmann, as he took the precious package from the hapless inventor, tied a sand-filled dummy to the parachute and dropped it overboard. Amid much excitement, the package fell to earth swiftly, the crowd below watching in anticipation. It hit the ground hard, spilling sand across a wide area of the landing field. The laughter in the control cabin increased.

Only one of the passengers on board the airship did not laugh. He was one of an extremely rare breed in 1914 – a professional parachute jumper. His displays always attracted a great deal of interest from spectators and were usually carried out with a parachute pre-attached below a hovering balloon. Today's performance would be unusual, as he would be jumping from the airship with a new type of parachute, the first of its kind.

Lehmann beckoned to the jumper: 'Your turn next'. Without hesitation, the parachutist stepped out of the doorway of the control car and into the air clutching his experimental package. Fearing that he had sent the man to his death, Lehmann watched anxiously as the man's body twisted and turned, falling to earth beneath the giant airship. The tiny figures waiting on the aerodrome below looked up in fascination.

As he watched the spectacle unfold, Lehmann thought he saw the jumper throw the package aside as if discarding it. However, with a loud crack the parachute opened into a large expanse of fabric enabling the jumper to glide to earth slowly and safely, much to the delight of the cheering crowd.

What Lehmann and others had witnessed that day was a demonstration of the first model pack-parachute. It was a

The Sachsen *on a commercial flight over Cologne.*

valuable invention that would enable flyers of all kinds to jump from any height in an emergency and have a reasonable chance of survival.

In early 1916, with airships contributing fully to the strategic bombing campaign over England, the German Naval Airship Division made it compulsory for Zeppelin crews to carry such parachutes. However, given the impact on airship weights – they could increase the baggage weight by as much as a ton – and the difficulty of finding effective and accessible storage for them, the carrying of parachutes was later declared optional rather than mandatory. In the event, most crews chose to take to the air without them, fearing, in any case, that they would certainly drown as a result of a parachute drop into the icy-cold North Sea. This was to prove a disastrous decision for many airship crews during the First World War, including the ill-fated crew of Zeppelin L48 in June 1917.

CHAPTER 2

England: No Longer an Island

In his 1927 account of Zeppelin air raids in the First World War, Captain Ernst Lehmann provided a frank view of the preparedness of the German General Staff in 1914 for an air war in which dirigibles would play a role. His view was that airships had not figured in any early war plans and he believed they had 'received very little thought as military weapons'. Whether this was an accurate assessment or not, the simple facts of the matter were that as war began, Germany had few army, navy or commercial airships to draw on and those that were available or nearing completion were ill-prepared for any military role.

This position would change rapidly and by the end of 1915 there would be a considerable appetite for using airships for offensive and defensive military purposes, and demand grew for the completed craft necessary to facilitate this. Twenty-six Zeppelins were built in 1915 and in January of that year, after some initial reluctance by the Kaiser, army and navy chiefs began to formulate plans for a bombing campaign against Britain using airships. Daily reports from the Western Front on the harsh realities of the war contributed to the growing public clamour in Germany for severe action against the enemy, in particular England. The old foe must be made to pay, and Britain's comfortable island situation across the Channel helped to increase the public demand for attacks by sea or air, hastening a speedy resolution to the conflict.

The threat of bombardment from the sea, and the fear of civilian casualties from this for the first time in centuries, created predictable unease among the British after early attacks on Great Yarmouth and Hartlepool. For the East Anglian population there was also the fear of coastal invasion. But of greater concern, for the first time in history, was the panic and alarm caused by the threat of air raids and, in particular, bombing by airships. Many in the British military held that air raids on civilian populations were not only immoral but also a violation of international law. In a paper entitled 'The Limitations of Aerial Bombardment by International Law', presented at the 44th annual meeting of the Aeronautical Society on 10 September 1909, Colonel F.G. Stone of the Royal Artillery claimed that aerial bombing was prohibited by such laws except as a method of breaking down the resistance of defended towns or destroying the enemy's war materials.

But in the emerging era of 'total war' the civilian population felt very vulnerable – the perception was that airships could attack effortlessly, protected by the cover of cloud, dropping large numbers of bombs unimpeded by either ground defences or fighter planes. While this threat would largely prove to be more apparent than real, such fears were not unfounded and it would take several months from the start of the war for air raid precautions, anti-aircraft batteries and well-equipped home defence squadrons to be established along the south and east coasts of England.

A postcard showing early ground defences in Suffolk. (Taken from the Illustrated Memorial of the Great War in relation to Leiston & District, *produced by local photographer John Smellie Waddell)*

A propaganda poster from 1914 illustrating the perceived threat from Zeppelin airships.

And yet the military use of airships was hardly a new concept. As early as 1670 a Jesuit priest by the name of Francesco de Lana-Terzi had written a scientific treatise in which he suggested that a boat-shaped carriage could be raised into the air by the lifting power of four large globes of very thin copper from which air had been extracted using pumps. He envisaged the terror that could be unleashed with such weapons, remarking that, 'No city can be secure against attack, since our ship may at any time be placed directly over it ...'. In his 1908 fictional novel *The War in the Air*, H.G. Wells described an airship attack on New York by German airships. In the book he foresaw that,

> The special peculiarities of aerial warfare were of such a nature as to trend, once it had begun, almost inevitably towards social disorganisation. The first of these peculiarities was brought home to the Germans in their attack upon New York; the immense power of destruction an airship has over the thing below...

German Zeppelins bombed Britain for the first time on 19 January 1915 and it was East Anglia that bore the brunt. High explosive bombs were dropped on Great Yarmouth and King's Lynn, killing four people – the first British citizens to die in an air raid. *The Times* described these attacks as bringing to an end 'the age-long immunity of the heart of the British Empire from the sight of a foe and the sound of an enemy missile'. The pattern of attacks on East Anglia, in particular, would become a consistent part of the air war on England, and of the fifty-one nights of air raids that occurred between January 1915 and August 1918 well over half involved airship raids on the region.

The German press was euphoric in its response to these early Zeppelin raids. A Leipzig newspaper announced: 'England no longer an island! The city of London, the heart which pumps the life-blood into the arteries of the brutal huckster nation, has been sown with bombs by German airships.' Elsewhere, whenever Count Zeppelin appeared in public, school children sang a popular and chilling song:

Great Yarmouth was the first town in Britain to be bombed by Zeppelin airships. On 19 January 1915 high explosive bombs were dropped on the undefended town, killing two people and destroying property.

Zeppelin, Flieg,
Hilf uns im krieg,
Flieg nach England,
England wird abgebrannt,
Zeppelin, Flieg.
(Zeppelin, Fly,
Help us win the war,
Fly against England,
England will be burned,
Zeppelin, Fly.)

In Britain there was vociferous public outrage at the air attacks, with the Germans being variously described in the press as 'baby-killers' and 'murderers of women'. Following an air raid in the Midlands in 1916, the *Nottingham Evening Post* on 3 February reported the views of a local coroner that the events were a 'dastardly outrage' and 'a piece of German frightfulness'. It went on to say, 'We were able to realise now the horrible character of the warfare which was being carried on against us and by what was once believed to be a civilised nation.'

Such views owed much to the hysteria of the times and the propaganda campaign that would become a consistent feature of this and every major war from 1914 onwards. The reality was that the nature of warfare had changed for good and Britain could no longer expect to fight battles on foreign soil without any disruption to the home population. In the latter months of 1916 Corvette Captain Peter Strasser, the Leader of Airships in the German Fleet Command, suggested that 'it was not upon the direct material damage that the value of the airship attacks depended, but rather on the general result of the German onslaught upon England's insularity otherwise undisturbed by war'. In a private letter he confessed,

We who strike the enemy where his heart beats have been slandered as 'baby-killers' and 'murderers of women'... What we do is repugnant to us too, but necessary. Very necessary. Nowadays there is no such animal as a non-combatant; modern warfare is total warfare. A soldier cannot function at the front without the factory worker, the farmer and all the other providers behind him.

It was clear from an early stage in the war that Britain's civilian population, whether in urban or rural communities, could expect changes and hardships unheard of prior to 1914. Feverish preparations, precautions and defensive provisions replaced the attempt at 'business as usual' in the early months of the war and the apparent air of normality was soon dissipated. The Defence of the Realm Acts of 1914, extended in 1915 and 1916, led to increased governmental control of individual freedoms covering a wide range of factors from travel to bank holidays, and introduced daylight time saving for the first time. Restaurants found it difficult to continue operating and food queues increased.

Civilians were becoming aware that they could no longer sit back and leave the war to the military – a fact brought home by the shelling of east coast towns in late 1914 and the start of the air raids in early 1915. Civilians and voluntary groups, keen to contribute to the war effort, handed over mufflers, mittens, hospital bags, bandages, books and cigarettes. And there was a certain irony in the fact that as men from cities, towns and villages all over Britain rushed to join up in the early part of the war for service overseas, few could have realised that within a matter of months bombs would be falling on their own homes and airships would become a familiar sight to many of the urban and rural communities they left behind.

Rural areas like East Anglia were not isolated from the growing demands of war. Men who were exempt from military service were enlisted into the Volunteers and National Guard to counter the threat of invasion. Many young women in Suffolk and elsewhere took up jobs working on farms or left their rural villages to work in factories, and in 1915 the first Women's Institute was founded, contributing in part to the need for increased home food production. In 1917 the Women's Land Army was created, enabling women to replace in the fields men who had enlisted.

There were other perceptible signs that country life had been disrupted. Military traffic on local roads and railways increased, troops were often billeted in rural homes, and in many parts of Suffolk the thunder and thud of guns on the Western Front could be heard on a regular basis. As food supplies ran short, prices rose and rationing was introduced. All of this increased the pressure to dig and cultivate more land in rural areas. Grassland was ploughed up, rural committees were set up to coordinate agricultural production, labour and machine pools were created, and in 1917 farmers were guaranteed grain prices for five years. In total, some 2 million acres of grassland were ploughed up and the production of wheat increased significantly.

However, it would be wrong to suggest that the war led to wholesale or widespread changes in all parts of the countryside and for many in isolated villages there was little disruption to everyday life. Many villages continued to have no gas, electricity, piped water or sewage disposal systems and roads were often poor, consisting of a top layer of flints collected in the fields and sold to local councils by farmers who were paid per tumbril load. In any case, road traffic remained comparatively light as a result of wartime petrol rationing and the fact that there were fewer than 200,000 cars nationally on the roads at that time. Most rural communities continued to be dependent on horse, pedal or foot power for their travel needs.

Ground defence and anti-aircraft preparations in East Anglia were as haphazard and inconsistent as other aspects of the military plan during the early part of the war. Fortuitously for the local population the Germans had no firm plans for air raids as hostilities commenced and had neither the aeroplanes nor the airships necessary to launch such attacks. However, for that brief period from the start of 1915, Germany's new airships were able to bomb the region with relative impunity. After the initial attacks on Great Yarmouth and King's Lynn in January of that year, further Zeppelin raids took place on Lowestoft, Bury St Edmunds, Ipswich and Harwich. The civilian population blacked out their windows and got used to the disruption that the aerial bombing caused. Some furnished hideaways in cellars or other parts of their homes. Most people had water or buckets of sand to hand in case of

An example of an early anti-aircraft gun of the sort used to attack raiding Zeppelin airships.

incendiary bombs. Over time, everyone began to take certain precautions.

Formal defences were slow in coming and were initially centred on urban targets and large ports. However, over time a network of anti-aircraft guns, searchlights and home defence squadrons was put in place along the Essex, Suffolk and Norfolk coastline. Other air raid precautions included sirens and a network of police and civilian volunteers to coordinate the response to an enemy attack. Several coastal regiments had their own cyclist battalions that patrolled their areas 'to prevent an enemy from landing unobserved and unreported'; they also reported 'anything unusual, particularly on the sea or in the sky'.

Once fully established, the home defence squadrons in the eastern region were to prove vital, alongside the searchlights and anti-aircraft batteries, in challenging the air supremacy of German Zeppelins. These squadrons formed part of the Royal Flying Corps (RFC) that had been constituted by Royal Warrant on 13 April 1912. But the air battle brought casualties on both sides. On 31 January 1916 nine Zeppelins flew across the North Sea and dropped 389 bombs over the Midlands, causing considerable damage. One of the Zeppelins crashed into the sea on its return and all sixteen of its crew members died.

Later that year sixteen German army and navy airships set off on a joint attack over eastern England on the largest raid ever mounted. Ten of the airships managed to cross the North Sea, reaching London at around midnight. Having dropped its bombs, one of the airships involved was chased by several aircraft and ran the gauntlet of heavy anti-aircraft fire, before being shot down over Hertfordshire by incendiary bullets from the machine-gun of an RFC pilot. As the airship fell to the ground in flames, its demise was witnessed by many thousands of people who watched with a mixture of horror, excitement, fear and enthusiasm. On 1 October 1916 a further raid by seven airships enabled the Germans to drop more than 200 bombs on Britain. However, another of the raiders was shot down by the RFC, this time at Potters Bar, and all nineteen of its crew died, including the charismatic and widely respected airship commander Heinrich Mathy. At last it seemed as if the tide was turning against Germany and the pre-eminence of its airship commanders.

Much of the continuing impetus for Germany's naval airship campaign came as a result of the energy, enthusiasm and single-minded determination of Peter Strasser, in his capacity as head of the Naval Airship Division. Strasser was a slim, darkly handsome man, always immaculately dressed and

Peter Strasser, Leader of Airships in the Naval Airship Division of the German Fleet Command.

coiffured, who sported the popular moustache and goatee beard so beloved of airship officers. He was charismatic, sharp and eloquent, inspiring ultimate loyalty among his officers and men and leading by example. Born in Hanover on 1 April 1876, he had joined the navy at 15, serving on the ships *Stein* and *Moltke* before entering the famous Naval Academy at Kiel. Strasser was quick to excel at all of the challenges presented to him, gaining promotion to lieutenant in 1897; while serving as a gunnery officer on the *Panther* in 1904 he won the *Kaiserpreis*, the award for the best artilleryman in the service.

Strasser had volunteered for duty as an aviator in 1911, but it was not until 1913, following the premature death of Corvette Captain Metzing, who was aboard the airship L1 when it crashed during a scouting mission near Heligoland on 9 September, that Strasser was offered the opportunity to lead the Naval Airship Division. From the moment of his appointment, he worked relentlessly and conscientiously to build an airship capability that could challenge the British home front and divert valuable military resources away from the battlefields of western Europe. His contributions to the development of Zeppelin airships were not just confined to the personnel and military-management role: he suggested and often tested many technical innovations; he lobbied the German Fleet Command on strategic and resource issues; and he regularly took to the air to lead midnight raids on Britain. His reputation, spirit and dedication won him the nickname 'the Kaiser' at the Division's Nordholz headquarters and on 20 August 1917 he was awarded the *Pour le Merite*, or 'Blue Max', Germany's highest decoration for gallantry – one of only forty-nine such awards given to navy personnel during the entire war.

In the late summer of 1916, with the growing losses of airships, the German Fleet Command debated whether to continue with the air campaign, the army having already abandoned its use of airships for attacks on England. But Strasser was combative, stressing the importance of tying up British military resources. In a communication to the Imperial Command of the German High Seas Fleet, he announced, 'The performance of the big airships has reinforced my conviction that England can be overcome by means of airships, inasmuch as the country will be deprived of the means of existence through increasingly extensive destruction of cities, factory complexes, dockyards, harbour works with war and merchant ships lying therein, railroads etc.' For the moment he was to win the debate, and the air raids continued, albeit fewer in number. However, he, like others, realised that continuing heavy losses could be expected until new and more effective ways of bombing could be established. From early 1917 Strasser was convinced that he had found such an approach and pinned his hopes on a new breed of airship, a design exemplified by Zeppelin L48.

CHAPTER 3

Launch Day at Friedrichshafen

For many years the town of Friedrichshafen on the northern bank of Lake Constance in southern Germany had been the principal centre of production for the thriving Zeppelin organisation. The company's early tests on airships during the late 1890s had been undertaken at a large and comparatively flat site outside the town near the village of Manzell. By July 1914, after four years of peacetime operations, Zeppelin's commercial airships had completed almost 1,600 flights carrying over 10,000 passengers and covering 107,000 miles. Enlargement of the original factory site at Friedrichshafen and the creation of a new factory at Potsdam would enable a vast expansion in the production of Zeppelin airships during the First World War, to the extent that one new airship could be produced every five to six weeks. By the end of the war there would be 1,600 technical staff and a workforce of 12,000 at Friedrichshafen and Lowenthal alone. The construction plant would be equipped to build the largest and most modern airships in the world, and laboratories, wind tunnels, engine-testing chambers and shops would spring up around the site to support the industry.

On 22 May 1917 a new type of Zeppelin emerged from the production facility at Friedrichshafen: naval airship L48 was the first of a series of dirigible aircraft known as 'height-climbers'. They were so called because they were capable of flying at altitudes of between 16,000ft and 20,000ft, crucially beyond the range of the ground-based anti-aircraft guns and fighter aircraft of the time. As a result of this and other innovations, these Zeppelins would push the boundaries of airship design in Germany and elsewhere. Later, after the turbulent years of the war, America would replicate the design of such height-climbers in the form of the star-crossed airship USS *Shenandoah*, which broke up and crashed in a severe

The Zeppelin works at Friedrichshafen where the L48 was constructed.

storm over Ohio on 3 September 1925. That airship was based
on Zeppelin L49, a sister-ship to the L48, which was captured
intact in France in October 1917 and later remodelled by the
Americans to use inert helium as its lifting gas.

The launch that day of the L48 was a sizeable operation.
The massive frame of the airship emerged slowly from its
construction hangar, Factory Shed 1, with over 300 ground
staff all around its bulk holding on to mooring lines to enable
the floating craft to be 'walked' carefully from its housing. The
only mechanical aids were the wheeled trolleys to which the
ship was attached to prevent it moving sideways in the wind
when entering or leaving the hangar. The trolleys moved on
docking rails that ran through the hangar and for 200 yards
out on to the airfield.

With an overall length of 645ft and a diameter of 78ft –
larger than any battleship of that time – this was a vision to
behold and the technical staff responsible for its creation

The L48 on a trial flight at Friedrichshafen.

observed its emergence with satisfaction and reverence. They watched as the front section of the Zeppelin came into view, its sizeable white L48 moniker adorning the side of the hull. At the same height, but just beyond the mid-section of the airship, they noted with pride the huge black and white imperial Iron Cross as it emerged from the construction hangar. Slung beneath the structure were four streamlined gondolas, representing the two amidship engine cars, a front control cabin and a rear engine car. The front and middle gondolas each contained a 240 horse-power Maybach engine connected to a propeller, while the single pusher propeller of the rear gondola was designed to be driven by two Maybach engines working in tandem.

Among the crowd of onlookers that day was the chief designer of the airship, Ludwig Dürr, whom the Zeppelin Company had hired as a young engineer in Stuttgart to undertake stress calculations on early airships. He was to remain the key technical figure within the organisation during the war years and beyond, working as chief designer on the construction of all but one of the 118 Zeppelins built, and eventually supervising the design and construction of Germany's commercial flagship, the *Graf Zeppelin*, in the late 1920s. From design to build, the L48 had taken four months to create and had involved a total of over 1 million direct man-hours of construction time. Its cost when built was DM3,264,000, or £163,000.

The outer skin of the airship was dark and foreboding, the nose, tail and lower hull sections painted in black aniline or 'dope' to reduce its visibility from the ground and thus lessen the threat from enemy searchlights. The upper sections were lighter in colour to minimise the impact of the sun as it warmed and expanded the almost 2,000,000ft^3 of hydrogen gas contained in the eighteen gas cells of the vessel. The 'goldbeaters' skin' of the gas cells was made from the lower intestines of oxen. The name was derived from the medieval period when expensive gold leaf had been produced by beating the metal between these thin animal skins. Overlapped into layers, the skins were able to grow together to form a homogenous covering which, when stuck with a rubber solution to the inside of cotton fabric, remained remarkably gastight. Each cell required as many as 50,000 skins, making them enormously expensive.

While these gas cells and the internal structural framework of the airship could not be seen from the outside, the skeleton was well known to all of those assembled who had worked night and day on the airship in recent weeks. The Zeppelin engineers had constructed the main rings and integral girders of the airship's framework from an aluminium alloy known as 'dural' (or duraluminium), chosen for its high strength-to-weight ratio. Its constituents were copper, magnesium and manganese, although over 90 per cent of the alloy was aluminium.

The assembled onlookers also knew that this vessel was the first to be built with a number of standard weight-saving features, some of which had been tested on earlier prototype airships, in support of its height-climbing aspirations. These included a reduction in the number of engines from six to five, the stripping of all non-essential baggage, a cutback in fuel-carrying capability, and the removal of some defensive weapons and ammunition. These modifications led to a weight saving of almost 25 per cent, and increased the 'useful lift' of the airship – the lift generated after subtracting the weight of the airship itself and its hydrogen – to nearly 86,000lb. Test flights carried out later that day would also reveal that even with the removal of one engine the trial speed of 66mph exceeded that of earlier airships.

Like all airships, the L48 was able to fly as a result of three types of lifting force: static lift, dynamic lift and powered dynamic lift. The most important of these was its static lift, the natural buoyancy created as a result of the hydrogen-filled gas cells being lighter than the surrounding air. This is the force on which balloonists have relied throughout the ages in ascending to the skies. However, unlike airships, balloons have no rudders to enable them to be steered and their static lift is largely inefficient in moving the craft through the air. The streamlined outer envelope and rear elevators of the L48 were carefully shaped to allow the airship's movement to generate dynamic lift in addition to its ability to float. Combined with the forward motion created by its engine-driven propellers, the airship was also able to benefit from powered dynamic lift in the same way as an aeroplane.

For the airship crew, however, this was not the end of the story. Airship flying required an excellent working knowledge of the weather and its likely effects. There was a wide range of influential factors, but the wind conditions, air pressure and temperature changes were all critical to airships. A strong headwind could prevent or hinder the movement of the airship along its intended route. As the airship climbed, its lifting gas would expand owing to the reduction in ambient air pressure, which steadily decreased the further the vessel rose from the earth's surface, requiring the valving off of some gas to prevent overpressure and to level out the differences in air pressure. Air temperature, particularly the warming effect of the sun, could also expand the lifting gas, increasing the displacement of air which results from the temperature of the hydrogen being higher than that of the surrounding air, and increasing the Zeppelin's static lift. Combined with the impact that rainwater and ice could have on the weight of the travelling airship and the potentially explosive effects of lightning strikes on the highly flammable gas cells, it was clear that airship flying was not for the faint-hearted.

After almost an hour of carefully planned manoeuvring the L48 stood on the extensive airfield site, south of the hangars, ready for launch. At the appointed moment the order was given for the multiple engines of the airship to be started up and the numerous mooring lines to be released. Within minutes the characteristic sound of heavy propellers thumping

One of the rolling trolleys used to bring airships out of the sheds at Nordholz.

the air could be heard across the factory, fields and landscape of the Friedrichshafen site – a sound that the local population had grown used to as the production of airships had been steadily stepped up to meet Germany's war demands. Almost effortlessly the Zeppelin rose into the air, a few tendrils of smoke drifting up and around the craft as a result of backfiring in the port engine, and climbed above the assembled launch party to the cheering and clapping of the multitude. This day was the culmination of many weeks of hard toil and meticulous planning by all concerned and the sense of pride was both palpable and predictable.

The following day the L48 was commissioned and flown to its permanent base at Nordholz in northern Germany, a journey which took just under 10 hours. Its new captain was the accomplished and devoted Lieutenant Commander Franz Georg Eichler of the Naval Reserve.

CHAPTER 4

'Attack South England – If Possible, London'

Saturday, 16 June 1917 dawned bright and clear. Continuing what the meteorologists referred to as a prolonged anti-cyclone, the weather across Britain and northern Germany proved to be unrelentingly hot. In parts of East Anglia the temperature reached 90°F in the shade and during the previous twenty-one years there had been only six warmer days recorded. For the German Naval Airship Division the outlook continued to be promising for a midnight attack on England, although with the shortest day less than a week away, the crews could expect only three hours of semi-darkness over their targets. And now there was a new, added impetus for demonstrating that the Division's airships could continue to contribute effectively to the air campaign – only three days before, Germany had launched its first successful bombing raid on London using Gotha aeroplanes.

Elsewhere, events were unfolding thick and fast. Although the United States had entered the war in April 1917, it was only in June that the first American ground troops had begun to arrive on the Western Front. As they did so, the British were launching a sustained attack at Messines in Flanders and in the air war above the trenches British and German fighter pilots were locked in mortal combat. On the Eastern Front Germany was making headway against the Russians and the Bolshevik revolution was beginning to take hold, with the first all-Russian Congress of Soviets beginning in Petrograd later that day – an event that was to signal the start of Russia's eventual withdrawal from the war. In the war at sea there was similarly no let up, and the day brought the torpedoing of the steamship *John D. Archbold* by a German submarine off the coast of Ushant, France, and the capture by the German raider *Wolf* of the schooner *Winslow* in the Pacific Ocean off Sunday Island.

Beyond the war, other events across the globe included the birth in New York of Katherine Graham, who was to become one of America's most famous and admired media figures, and the publisher of the *Washington Post* during the Watergate scandal of the early 1970s.

The German airship base at Nordholz on the North Sea coast was the largest of a number of airfields established by the Naval Airship Division for its wartime raids and reconnaissance work. Others were set up at Ahlhorn, Hage, Tondern and Wittmundhaven. Nordholz also served as the Division's headquarters and played host to both Peter Strasser and Hugo Eckener. The latter had joined the Zeppelin Company in 1909 as its first full-time Director of Public Relations, and went on to become the driving force behind the organisation's commercial operations in the 1920s and 1930s and the future commander of the globe-trotting airship *Graf Zeppelin*. At the outbreak of war Eckener, already a respected and highly skilled airship commander, was given the honorary rank of lieutenant commander and placed in charge of the training school at Nordholz. He was nicknamed 'the Pope' by the men he trained, as his meteorological predictions proved to be unerringly accurate.

Lying to the south of Cuxhaven in a vast open area near the village of Nordholz, the base was largely unappealing to the officers, crew and ground staff based there. The predominantly rural base was close to a small railway station

The Nordholz airship base in northern Germany.

and a pine wood, and lacked all but the most basic of amenities. The officers lived in army huts and spent much of their time in the officers' mess, or *Kasino*, with its comfortable surroundings and seafaring paintings. The crews lived in the airship sheds, where they were expected to maintain a constant state of readiness. Off duty the men drank at the railway restaurant.

Originally purchased in 1912 at an equivalent cost of £83,400, the base was developed throughout the war and by 1918 contained five sheds in addition to the famous 625ft-long revolving hangar, weighing 4,000 tons, which enabled the launching of airships according to the most favourable wind direction. The sheds were all given names beginning with 'No' – Nobel, Normann, Nora, Norbert, Nogat and Nordstern. The L48 was housed in the 787ft-long Normann shed, which had been completed on 26 April 1916 and could accommodate eight large and two small Zeppelins. It had huge rolling doors at both ends and its own underground petrol store capable of holding 7,926 gallons of fuel.

The famous revolving airship shed at Nordholz.

In addition to the administrative buildings, living quarters and hangars, the site contained a gas works, gasometer and chimney for producing the precious hydrogen on which the airships depended, as well as the twin towers of the wireless station, an anti-aircraft battery and a mooring mast. There was also a flight of defending aeroplanes, and captive balloons hovering above the airfields that were used to signal to crews landing in fog. Supporting the airship operations was a permanent ground staff of around 1,300 men known affectionately by all as the 'Nordholz acrobats'.

In a period when most German soldiers, sailors and civilians were experiencing severe food shortages and other material hardships, in part as a result of British naval blockades, airship crews were relatively well supplied and few of their food items were rationed. Both inside and outside the service, the Naval Airship Division was viewed as an elite unit, a factor that helped to promote a strong sense of camaraderie and collaboration among airship officers and crewmen. Perception was as important as reality. Ernst Lehmann best summed it up when he described the airship crews as 'a distinctly individual group of men, who, if not cast in a more heroic mould than the others, were entitled to the utmost consideration, for the chances were against their returning from a flight over the enemy'. The reality was that service on an airship required a particularly high level of specialist technical knowledge, bravery and physical strength. As a result, most personnel were specially selected or recruited for service and crews were awarded a high level of military honours – almost all officers received the Iron Cross, as did any crew member who participated in a raid over Britain.

Despite the long daylight hours and limited cover of darkness, Peter Strasser took the decision to launch a raid on Britain that Saturday, planning midnight attacks on the south of England. As was customary, however, the chosen airship commanders were not told in advance what their targets were – in fact, their sealed orders were usually opened only when the Zeppelins were airborne and heading out across the North Sea. The raiding party that day was to consist of the L42, L44, L45, L46, L47 and L48, with the latter acting as the lead airship of the fleet. Only the L42, commanded by Martin

Commander of the L48, Lieutenant Franz Eichler (centre), along with colleagues from the Naval Airship Division.

Dietrich, and the L48 under Franz Georg Eichler would be launched from Nordholz.

Throughout the morning the sunlight continued to stream down across the base and the heat of the day increased

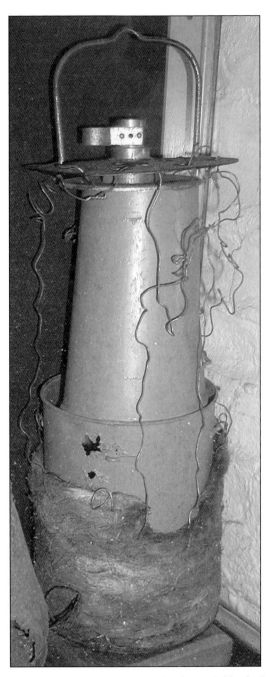

An example of the type of incendiary bombs carried by the L48.

The 645ft-long L48 in flight.

steadily. The large expanse of blue sky was adorned with occasional, pure white cumulus clouds. The conditions for take-off were almost perfect, with only a breath of wind to freshen the air.

In traditional style Dietrich and Eichler spent part of the morning in the *Kasino* talking to fellow officers, speculating on the raid that evening and preparing themselves mentally for the task ahead. They were joined by Corvette Captain Viktor Schütze, who on 23 November 1916 had assumed the role of overall commander of the Naval Airship Division, acting as deputy to Strasser who had been promoted to 'Leader of Airships' in the German Fleet Command. Schütze was to fly on board the L48 and act as the senior airship officer coordinating the raid. Born in Hanover on 6 March 1878, and a member of an old local business family, Schütze was in fact married to an Englishwoman. But as a veteran airship commander he had flown in numerous raids across Britain in airships like the L48 and L36. He had passed command of the L36 over to Eichler on 9 December 1916 when he received his promotion. But after the loss of the L36 in an operational accident during February 1917, the crew had been transferred to the newly commissioned L48. Schütze would therefore be flying in familiar and trusted company.

This was the L48's first bombing mission, the airship having been engaged mainly in test flights and height trials since being commissioned, although its operational record already included four scouting missions. Alongside its ability to fly into the sub-stratosphere, the airship had another key attribute – its operational range, which would allow the craft to fly for many hours across the North Sea to attack Britain and return to Germany without refuelling.

The crews of the L42 and L48 busied themselves in the sheds, preparing the Zeppelins for action. Having returned from a mission, it was normal practice for a large rigid airship to be deflated and suspended from the roof of its hangar by large slings. This prevented damage to the control and engine cars. The crews and ground staff inflated and checked each gas cell, repairing any damage found on the outer coverings – among other problems it was not unknown for the goldbeaters' skin to be eaten by mice. The ground staff also used fire ladders to check and mend any damage to the outer covering, or envelope, of the hull.

The precious hydrogen, the lightest of all gases, was drawn from the on-site gas plant. In the early days of lighter-than-air travel, the gas had been made by passing sulphuric acid over iron filings or zinc in lead-lined barrels, the acid spray being removed by allowing the gas to pass through water. However, the resultant product was largely impure, containing quantities of hydrogen sulphide and residual acid. Germany was later to employ the Messerschmitt Process, producing hydrogen from the passage of steam over heated iron turnings. This was the method employed at the Nordholz gas plant, producing 1,060,000ft^3 of hydrogen each day. The gas was stored in 150 large underground steel cylinders and in an above-ground low-pressure gas container – the field in front of which was constantly scorched.

Within the light, cathedral-sized interior of the Normann shed, the L48 was prepared for take-off. Drums of engine fuel and lubricating oil were loaded into the inner skeleton. Machine-guns were mounted in the control car and heavy boxes of ammunition placed alongside them. Water was taken on board for drinking and to fill rubberised ballast sacks in the bottom of the hull, each holding 2,200lb of water mixed with anti-freeze. Additional smaller sacks of water ballast, known as 'breeches', were also filled at the nose and tail of the craft, to enable the ship to be lightened quickly during take-off or landing. Medical supplies and other specialist equipment were checked and replaced. The provisions for the crew included *kaloritkonserven* – tinned meats, hashes and stews that could be heated upon opening by a chemical process, thus removing the need for cooking with a dangerous naked flame. There was also plenty of black bread and good butter, chocolate, thermos flasks filled with extra strong coffee and alcohol flasks containing an allowance of brandy or rum for each man. The latter could only be opened once the airship had ascended to at least 10,000ft. Should this height not be achieved on the mission, Commander Eichler would expect every man to return a full flask.

Despite their superstitious nature as sailors, and the fact that this was to be their thirteenth mission, the crew elected, as they always had, not to stow pack-parachutes on board that day because of the adverse effect on the airship's weight. They did, however, hoist the traditional war ensign to bring them luck.

Just before midday the final preparations were made for the movement of the L48 to its launch site on the airfield. Schütze stood alongside Eichler in the control car, together with the airship's navigator, Paul Westphal, and the helmsmen in charge of the elevator and rudder controls. The executive officer, Lieutenant Otto Mieth, supervised the withdrawal of the airship on the ground. As the watch officer, he assumed the general responsibility for the airship's crew, reporting to Commander Eichler.

With its nineteen crew on board the airship was weighed-off. With great precision, the crew sought to adjust the weight of the craft so that it floated perfectly with the correct trim. The elevator man valved-off 550lb of water ballast to lighten the craft and the balance of weight between the stern and bow sections was checked to ensure the correct pitch. With an approving nod from Eichler, Mieth gave the order for the Zeppelin to be walked from the shed attached to the rolling trolleys on the docking rails and assisted by over 300 ground staff. Some pulled on the numerous mooring lines attached to the nose and keel, others grasped the handling rails beneath the gondolas, and very slowly the airship began to be manoeuvred from the hangar.

In the heat and glare of the midday sun the Nordholz station band accompanied the movement of the war machine with a rendition of 'The Admiral of the Air'. But as the music resonated across the airfield and echoed around the station buildings, the intense heat of the summer sun dramatically cracked the skin of the big drum from top to bottom. Some of the crew saw this as an ill omen, a sign they would have preferred not to witness.

At its launch position the L48 hovered regally above the airfield, its massive size and shape casting a huge dark shadow across the ground handlers below. Mieth shouted for the multitude of mooring lines to be released. The men holding the handling rails below the gondolas then released their grip and the craft floated steadily upwards. From the control car Commander Eichler gave the order for the five Maybach engines to be started up inside the gondolas and within a couple of minutes the roar of the powerful engines and rhythmical whirring of the wooden propellers created an almost orchestral harmony across the base. Mieth waved his hand to the Nordholz acrobats and shouted a spirited, 'Back tomorrow!' as the airship rose higher and higher into the air. At a height of a few hundred feet the engines were engaged and given full throttle and Zeppelin L48 left Nordholz on a course for the coast and the North Sea route towards England.

In an 1887 report to the King of Wurttemburg, Count Zeppelin had stressed that if an airship was to be useful for military matters it would have to be manoeuvrable in the face of powerful air currents, able to remain in the air without landing for at least 24 hours and designed to carry a sizeable load of men, ammunition and supplies. The L48 was the newborn realisation of that vision and an awe-inspiring weapon of war. As Lieutenant Franz Georg Eichler controlled the flight of the airship that day he carried with him the hopes and expectations of all commanders that his Zeppelin could help to bring a decisive end to the war. Equally strong in Eichler's mind was his desire for the mission to run smoothly, without any of the operational difficulties that had so beset combat Zeppelins in previous weeks and months. Only two days before, the Ahlhorn-based L43 had been shot down by British aircraft with the loss of all twenty-four of its crewmen.

Eichler was born in Giebichenstein, near the town of Halle in Saxony, on 29 October 1877. He had joined the Naval Reserve in Hamburg on 2 April 1895 and was promoted to the rank of lieutenant on 8 February 1908. Serving with the Hamburg–Amerika shipping line prior to the war, he had been captain of the *Vaterland* and *Imperator*, the latter being the world's largest ship at the time. Little did he know that his planned career as a seafaring officer would lead him to become one of a small but select band of commanders in the Naval Airship Division.

Having earlier flown on the L13, Eichler took over command of the airship L36 in December 1916. But with only one aborted raid and four reconnaissance flights to its credit,

The SS Imperator, *captained by Franz Eichler before the war, and once the largest ship in the world.*

the L36 crashed after a forced landing in the iced-up River Aller, near Rethem, on 7 February 1917. The airship had run into difficulties after taking off from Nordholz on the previous evening and Eichler had struggled valiantly to maintain control of the craft before it finally descended into the river having lost all of its ballast and fuel and most of its lifting gas. A Court of Inquiry set up to investigate the circumstances surrounding the crash concluded that although Eichler had made two errors of judgement he should be absolved of blame. Strasser was strongly supportive of Eichler in his contribution to the Inquiry: 'Considering that the commander did not abandon his badly damaged ship for one moment, but on the contrary, courageously strove to bring his ship home, and in consideration of his previous blameless airship record as well as his war service, I have no hesitation in entrusting him with the command of another airship.' And so, on the afternoon of 16 June 1917, Eichler stood at the helm of the L48 on its first mission to attack England.

The Zeppelin flew at a height of less than 1,000ft on its short course towards the coast, its engines maintaining full throttle as directed by Eichler. The landscape of the Upper Saxony region continued to unfold, its sandy lowlands and dykes, which acted as a natural barrier to flooding from the sea, etched out clearly below the airship. While attentive to any perceptible changes in the climate, Eichler and Schütze were confident for the moment that the early weather predictions from the ground were good for the raid.

Having cleared the coastline, Eichler gave orders for the bombs on board the airship to be prepared for action. This required the rigger to turn the ignition pins around on the thick-walled, pear-shaped missiles that were carried in racks on either side of the hull amidships. The Zeppelin also carried a number of incendiary bombs made of thermite wrapped in tarred rope.

The L48 headed out over the sea, maintaining a height of only a few hundred feet. Commander Eichler then proceeded to open his sealed orders from Peter Strasser. As ever, these were short and to the point, 'Attack south England – if possible, London.' This perceived vagueness owed much to

Strasser's confidence in his officers that while broad objectives were needed for each raid, it was up to the commander to make the precise and final decisions at the point of attack based on the operational state of the airship, the prevailing climatic conditions and the degree of enemy resistance.

Within the radio cabin of the control car a message was received for Corvette Captain Schütze. This alerted him to the fact that the airships L46 and L47 had been confined to their sheds at Ahlhorn owing to strong winds. The L48 continued to cruise over the Heligoland Bight before making rendezvous with the remainder of the raiding party. This was the traditional assembly point for airships from the various German stations, and as the afternoon sun beamed down across the vast expanse of sea, the four giant airships hung in the air like a gathering of storm clouds. Schütze led the exchange of coded signals between the airships, ensuring that all were clear about the mission ahead. The airships then set off in a loose formation steering westward.

At this stage the radio traffic between the airships and ground stations was relatively heavy, with coded bearings being sent to the crews every half an hour. But as the long flight across the North Sea continued and the threat of interception from radio operators in the British Naval Intelligence Division increased, the airship commanders kept to a minimum their contacts with the outside world.

As the airships continued to head in a westerly direction they passed the coastal port of Wilhelmshaven away to their left. A number of ships from the Imperial Germany Navy, lying at watch in the Schillig Roads, signalled for the crews to have 'a successful trip'. The airships then lost sight of the North Frisian Islands and their homeland began to disappear slowly behind them. All that faced them now was the steady, familiar journey across the North Sea, with all eyes trained on the sky and water ahead.

Throughout the vessel the crew worked diligently at their stations to maintain the speed and smooth running of the airship. The rigger made sure that the gas cells were not punctured or losing gas. The engineers maintained a watchful eye on the Maybach engines, ensuring that sufficient fuel reached the machines from the 44-gallon gravity tanks above the gondolas – the tanks being filled by hand-pumping petrol from slip tanks held within the hull. As the airship climbed, the engines would often become starved of oxygen and were prone to breakdowns or reductions in power. Oil and coolant lines were liable to freeze and component parts sometimes became brittle and fractured. At frequent intervals the engineers sent reports to the control car about the operation of the engines.

Conditions for the crew were basic. Along the bottom of the hull, running the complete length of the craft, was the structure containing the fuel tanks and water ballast bags and a walkway providing access to all parts of the airship. The gas cells took up over 90 per cent of the space within the hull and provision for the crew consisted of hammocks slung along the sides of the walkway or in any space that could be found between the gas cells and aluminium girders.

The crew laboured against a constant backdrop of noise, the monotonous drone of the engines and whirring of the 17ft-diameter propellers making it necessary for them to shout loudly or gesture in sign language to make themselves understood. To combat the freezing temperatures on board they wore thick woollen underwear beneath their naval kit, together with leather overalls, thick scarves and heavy, fur-lined overcoats. For extra warmth some resorted to an additional layer of newspapers beneath their overalls and all wore thick fur gloves, goggles and skullcaps. To complete the outfit they donned tall boots with large felt overshoes. Some had binoculars hung around their necks.

To counter the effects of altitude and the perils of altitude sickness, the crew also had access to thick-walled cylinders of liquid oxygen. In the early days of the war the men had been given compressed oxygen canisters, but many had refused to use them as the oxygen tasted musty, being contaminated with quantities of glycerine.

In the starboard engine car Machinist's Mate Heinrich Ellerkamm was, as ever, vigilant in his duties. Only a short time before he had climbed the thirteen rungs of the ladder leading from the car into the hull of the ship to pump enough fuel into the gravity tank to last until 6.00am. The hard-working engineer had flown many times with Commander Schütze in raids over England and had enjoyed a fair amount of good luck. He had been an airshipman since October 1914 and a regular crew member on the L19 until it crashed, killing all of the crew – Ellerkamm having given up his place to a colleague in the maintenance group who was keen to earn the customary Iron Cross for completing a raid on England. With his blond hair and blue eyes, the young Heinz was classically German. Back home he had become engaged to his sweetheart Gretel, who was eager to see him and enjoy the two weeks' leave that Ellerkamm had planned after the raid.

The engine in the control car, with its thick tubular exhaust pipe, was running smoothly and Ellerkamm was, for the moment, cosy in his thick overcoat and felt overshoes. The thermometer in the car showed that conditions were still relatively temperate, although Ellerkamm knew from experience that this would not last. He cast a glance out of the window of the car and saw only a clear blue sky and the choppy waves of the grey sea far below. Alongside him worked Machinist's Mate Wilhelm Uecker, although the two had barely spoken to each other since taking off owing to the tremendous and continuous roar of the engine beside them.

In the control car Eichler was vigilant on all fronts: ensuring that the airship maintained the required height, direction, speed and trim; studying the horizon for any signs of enemy activity; responding to radio messages and the various reports from his men; alert to every indication of climatic change. A sudden change in wind direction, a brisk build-up of cloud cover or rapid changes in either air temperature or pressure might signal difficulties ahead. But Eichler was not alone. Schütze, Mieth, Westphal and all of the crew that had any degree of visibility watched for the signs, alert and attentive during those long-drawn-out hours across the sea. Familiarity and experience had not diminished for one moment their acute and in-built feel for the way the airship was performing, the direction in which weather fronts were moving and the extent to which they were vulnerable to attack.

As the L48 approached the Dutch island of Terschelling, Eichler gave the order for the airship to ascend. The rudder helmsman acted accordingly and the Zeppelin began to climb steadily through the thin layer of cloud. As it did so the crew left behind the warm feel of summer and began to experience the thin air and icy chill of altitude. Gone was the warming effect of the summer sun, its heat replaced by a numbing coldness. The L48 was now in the danger zone and within range of enemy guns. Eichler was taking no chances. In recent days the British had attacked and destroyed two airships on reconnaissance flights in this area. Tired eyes anxiously scanned the horizon on the lookout for enemy aircraft and the conversation within the control car was kept to a minimum.

Beyond Terschelling the tension eased and very soon the raiding party was leaving the Dutch coast behind. The airships continued to fly high, but sighted no boats on the sea below. During the late afternoon the clouds were tinged with a fiery red and the airships began to break from their loose line of formation in preparation for the attack on London. The L44 and L45, which had both suffered from repeated engine failures across the North Sea, were forced to return to their bases, the L44 having to fly across Holland with only the port gondola engine working. This left only the L42 and L48 to continue the mission. Commander Dietrich aboard the L42 planned to attack London from the south, and ordered his navigating officer to set course for the south coast where the airship could make landfall between Dover and Dungeness. Eichler also hoped to cross the English coast at a point that would prevent detection by either the anti-aircraft guns or home defence squadrons.

The L48 pushed on into the early evening, the officers resigning themselves to the tedium of the North Sea, the rhythmical humming of the engines and the whistling of the propellers. A thin mist appeared above the sea and the sky began to darken as shafts of sunlight played fleetingly upon the waves far below.

CHAPTER 5

Zeppelins Over the Coast

The River Ore in East Suffolk runs parallel to the North Sea coastline for several miles, forming a peninsula of shingle and marshland with its neck at the seaside fishing port of Aldeburgh. In this largely untouched part of East Anglia the war had made less impact than in other parts of the country. There were some food shortages, but with game, fish and farm produce near at hand, life remained pretty much undisturbed. The main threat to the tranquillity of the area came from the nearby Orfordness lighthouse which, from the early days of the war, had become a natural sighting point for Zeppelin raiders.

Midway through the war another development brought the conflict closer to home. The RFC Experimental Station at Orfordness was established at the end of 1916 to develop, test and pioneer new ideas and innovations in aeroplane technology. The professor leading the research programme had assembled a small team of talented engineering graduates, together with a number of experienced pilots who were able to fly the aircraft stationed there. The airfield was situated on the marshes of the peninsula, accessible only by boat over 200 yards of tidal water, and prone to seasonal flooding. Under the station commander, Major P.C. Cooper, the facility operated primarily in its experimental capacity, but was also able to provide some measure of coastal defence, being equipped with aircraft, machine-guns and the latest explosive and incendiary ammunition. Its pilots were mobilised during airship attacks alongside men from the home defence squadrons.

Among the RFC pilots stationed at Orfordness in June 1917 were Second Lieutenant Frank Holder, who commanded A Flight, and Captain Robert Saundby, who commanded C Flight. Both officers had served in the same wing in France, flying offensive patrols over the Somme during some of the most active phases of the battle. On one occasion Saundby had saved Holder from the German ace Oswald Boelcke, driving the enemy plane off Holder's tail in a dogfight over St Quentin, and sustaining in the event a flesh wound in the elbow. In later life Holder was to describe Saundby as 'a brilliant pilot quite without fear'.

Frank Douglas Holder was born in London on 26 June 1897. After completing school, he was accepted into Sandhurst where he became a prize cadet. In January 1916 Holder was granted a commission as a second lieutenant in the RFC, having successfully applied to join the machine-gun corps. His initial posting was at Farnborough, but he later finished his training at Mousehold in Norfolk before seeing active service in France. Holder arrived at Orfordness on 1 January 1917 and became an active member of the research team, carrying out the first use of oxygen apparatus and electrically heated clothing in the air, alongside numerous tests on machine-guns, sights, ammunition, photography and pyrotechnics – the latter including trials of parachute flares, crucially requiring Holder's aeroplane to be equipped for night-flying.

By contrast, Robert Henry Magnus Spencer Saundby was born in Birmingham on 26 April 1896 and was educated at the city's St Edward School. He first served as a second lieutenant in the Royal Warwickshire Regiment, before being promoted to lieutenant and seconded as a flying officer in the RFC to serve in France and then Orfordness. His unit in France was the first single-seater fighter squadron to go to any battlefront and was commanded initially by Britain's first air ace, Major Lanoe George Hawker VC. It was while serving under Hawker that Saundby had one of his many brushes with death.

On 23 November 1916 he had been flying at the controls of his de Havilland biplane, in close formation with similar DH2 planes being flown by Hawker and other colleagues, as part of a routine patrol over the French countryside and the trenches and battle-lines of the Western Front. As the pilots undertook their reconnaissance, they spotted a number of German two-seater planes flying towards them in the distance. The British planes sought to close in, but the enemy cluster began to turn away from them, heading back towards German territory. Before any engagement could take place, the British pilots were attacked by a group of German single-seater fighters that dived on them from above. After some frantic manoeuvring, three of the planes managed to lose their pursuers and headed for their own lines, although Hawker continued to be tailed closely by one of the German fighters. For several minutes the two planes were locked in combat with Hawker rapidly firing rounds from his Lewis machine-gun and the German responding in kind. Then, in a decisive movement, Hawker broke away from the encounter and opened up the throttle to escape. The German pilot was quick to respond and tailed Hawker, gaining on him steadily. As he attempted to fire on the vulnerable plane, the German's machine-guns jammed, but relentlessly he continued the pursuit, retrying his weapons until at last he was able to fire several rounds into the British plane. Under the onslaught a bullet hit Hawker in the head, killing him instantly, and the DH2 spiralled out of control and down towards the ground. Saundby had had a lucky escape that day – the German pilot that had killed his commander with such deadly skill was none other than Manfred von Richthofen, the 'Red Baron'.

While there was no official rota for home defence duties at the Orfordness station, the facility tried to maintain a reasonable state of readiness for any incursions by enemy airships. But as the heavily armed L48 was crossing the North Sea on that Saturday afternoon, the men stationed at Orfordness were enjoying their only free period of the week and making the best of the perfect summer weather. Tenders ran to Ipswich, the largest town nearby, and the men pursued their own interests and hobbies. Holder, who often sailed on the River Ore with friends, was playing tennis at Sudbourne, a couple of miles from Orford.

Neither Saundby nor Holder could have envisaged the drama that lay ahead of them that night. And perhaps there was a certain irony in the fact that as each was called upon to take to the air in defence of their country, both would be flying the same type of aircraft they had flown in France over the Somme when they had attacked kite balloons.

In the radio cabin of the L48, Wilhelm Meier, a 22-year-old wireless operator from Meitzendorf, was busy sending and receiving messages and requesting cross-bearings prior to the attack using his powerful transmitter and receiver. At 8.30pm the L48 was less than 100 miles from the English coast. To determine the location of his airship, Eichler was reliant on dead reckoning – making use of any visible landmarks and a largely inaccurate system of bearings based on radio contact with the ground stations in the German Bight and Bruges, and translating this information to a map on his chart table using drawing pins and thread. This approach to navigation was not only imprecise, leading to consistently inaccurate bombing, but often alerted British radio operators to the imminent attacks.

Meier was the only trained wireless operator on board the airship. He sat alone for long periods in his narrow, soundproofed radio cabin in front of the engine but at the rear of the control car, listening to the busy radio traffic through his earphones. The cabin had a door and a low slender window enabling Meier to look out over the brooding North Sea. Aside from his radio paraphernalia, the only other equipment in the cabin was a barometer and a small altimeter showing the airship's height.

The ground stations at Tondern, List, Nordholz, Borkum and Bruges transmitted a regular flow of news, reports and orders alongside the navigational cross-bearings. Meier listened to these against a constant hail of atmospheric crackles and pops, making precise interpretation difficult. A crucial part of his role was to pick up the frequent weather reports, deciphering these with his 'weather key' and writing them down on a weather chart for Executive Officer Mieth – the latter acting as the main link with the control car, requesting bearings, passing on the messages to be sent and deciphering the various reports that came through from the ground. Meier's only breaks came when the radio aerial of the craft was withdrawn during raids and thunderstorms, when he was able to leave the cabin and stand alongside the officers controlling the airship.

At the front of the 34ft-long control car Eichler surveyed the darkening view ahead and watched over the operation of the airship. The vessel's navigational aids included a small liquid compass, a simple altimeter, a thermometer and an airspeed meter. There was also a small chart room on the port side. Communications with the rest of the ship were maintained through a primitive telephone system and by word of mouth, as members of the crew came and went via the ladder from the control car into the hull of the ship. There were also engine telegraph controls to change the running speed of the motors,

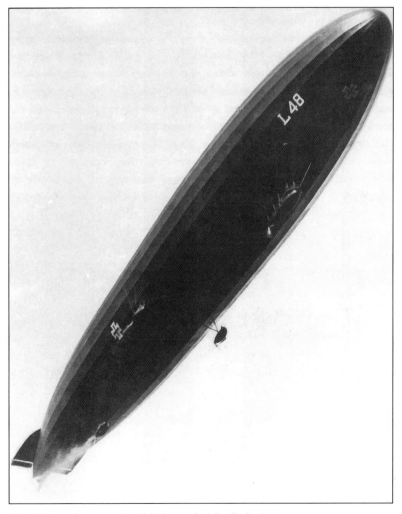

The L48 was known to the British as a 'height-climber'.

levers to open the manoeuvring valves of the individual gas cells, wires controlling the ballast containers and the all-important elevator and rudder wheels on the port and starboard sides of the cabin respectively. The latter were

Inside the rear engine car of a Zeppelin airship.

crucial to the smooth running of the vessel, the helmsmen needing a steady and experienced feel for the way the airship was moving. This was particularly critical for the L48 which had sacrificed much of the structural strength of earlier airships to achieve high-altitude flying – its designers had even recommended cautious use of the elevator and rudder controls at the lowest of altitudes.

Commander Schütze and navigator Paul Westphal, a 30-year-old from Insterburg, also paid close attention to the visibly changing conditions, knowing from the weather reports received earlier that storm clouds were gathering over Britain. It was still too early to make landfall, with the sky approaching only a twilight glow, and the L48 steered away from the land to wait for darkness. It also started to climb in an attempt to pass above the impending rain clouds. At 16,000ft a strong crosswind buffeted the airship and the light within the control car began to fade quickly. All at once the skies ahead were lit up with brilliant silver lightning streaks and deep thunder rumbled in the distance. With its lethal cargo of inflammable gas, Eichler was keen to avoid the blackening storm clouds and the L48 continued to fly above the clouds and out of range of the worst of the weather.

Heavy rainstorms were now sweeping over England. Vivid and continuous lightning and loud peals of thunder broke over the southern and eastern counties. In Norwich the storms continued uninterrupted for two hours. In London the rain fell exceptionally heavily – the downpour in the Shepherds Bush area was so severe that water flowed into the central tube system and caused a temporary stoppage of trains. In other parts of the capital thoroughfare drains were flooded and water mains burst on to stretches of road causing delays to tramway traffic.

The L42 had also encountered the edge of the storm. At 8.30pm the 645ft-long airship had been only 40 miles from Southwold on the Suffolk shoreline. Commander Dietrich had been content to hold the Zeppelin off the coast to avoid the worst ravages of lightning, hail and thunder, eventually passing through the storm without damage. But when the airship resumed its course he discovered that the direction of the wind had changed, and a strong headwind had begun to hamper their progress towards London. Dietrich later received a radio message from Schütze in the L48 saying, 'Weather good for London. Attack and departure course between east and north.' But while the L42 made its landfall between Dungeness and Dover as planned, the continuing headwind proved too strong and with insufficient time to attack the primary objective, Dietrich took the decision to bomb the port of Dover instead.

By this stage the L48 was also fighting the strong south-westerly gale, making its passage difficult. The continued high-altitude flying had begun to take its toll on the crew, the temperature having fallen by 72°F since they left Nordholz. As they shivered in their heavy clothing, breathing with some difficulty in spite of their oxygen supplies, several of the men became clumsy and sluggish, gripped by the first warning signs of anoxia (a shortage of oxygen in the blood). The mixture of alcohol and water in the ship's magnetic compass had also frozen, its disk looking like an ice slide. Despite his navigational problems and some difficulties in keeping his bearings, Eichler continued to drive the engines at full power until the starboard propeller stopped and Heinz Ellerkamm subsequently reported that the engine had broken down. Within a short time knocking could also be heard from the forward motor and Eichler reined back on the engines as the airship drifted towards the English coast.

After a lengthy debate, and in view of the continuing difficulties facing the airship, Schütze and Eichler decided to abandon the attack on London. They opted instead to bomb the Essex port of Harwich, which now lay less than 40 miles ahead wrapped in a thin layer of fog. The time was 11.34pm.

The coastal defence stations in East Anglia were already aware that an airship attack was under way. From September 1916 the Naval Intelligence Division in Whitehall had mastered the art of intercepting the wireless messages sent by raiding German airships and was able to forewarn both the ground and air defence networks. Given the crudity of wireless communications at that time, it has often been said that the British had a better idea of the position of an attacking airship than its crew. At around 10pm that Saturday evening the warning of an air raid had been sounded and the home defence squadrons and anti-aircraft batteries soon stood ready for action. In the wider community the police and special constables had been alerted and emergency preparations began to be made.

Major Cooper at the Orfordness station received the initial field marshal's warning at 9.58pm and the station stood ready for action some fifteen minutes later. At 10.50pm the further order 'Take air raid action' had been received. Sentries were posted at the base and those pilots that were available were placed on alert. Second Lieutenant Holder had just returned to the station when the first warning was received and he was immediately instructed to stand by to fly a Farman Experimental (FE2b) fighter against any sighted attackers. Sergeant Sydney Ashby was chosen to accompany him as observer and gunner, as the regular officers from the machine-gun section, Musson and Mackerrow, were not available. In any case Ashby was a capable section sergeant with more than enough experience of the machine-guns that the FE2b would be carrying – he had flown in a number of earlier flights trying them out.

Holder's plane, with its 160 horse-power, six-cylinder, water-cooled Beardmore engine, was the first to be built by the local firm of Ransomes, Sims & Jefferies. When it was completed, he had flown it over the factory in Fore Hamlet, Ipswich, to the delight of the staff who had laboured on its production. As the need had developed at Orfordness, the plane had been equipped for experimental work at night – in fact the Farman Experimental was the standard night-flying machine in France. Being a two-seater 'pusher-type', the plane had good forward visibility but at this stage in the war was considered slow in both overall speed and rate of climb. It was armed with two .303 calibre Lewis machine-guns with double drums, mounted on the plane to give the widest possible field of fire.

To feed the Lewis machine-guns the FE2b carried eight drums of Pomeroy, Brock and Buckingham ammunition, a combination known as 'mixed ammo'. It was only a year before that these new forms of ammunition had become accessible for general use when the Ministry of Munitions had purchased over a million rounds in the spring of 1916. The Brock and Pomeroy were explosive bullets named after their inventors, while the Buckingham was a phosphorous incendiary bullet. On their own, the three types of bullet were only marginally effective against an enemy airship. But in combination, they were devastating – the explosive bullets pierced the gas cells of a Zeppelin, enabling the combustible hydrogen to leak out and creating a volatile mixture with the oxygen in the air. The Buckingham rounds could then ignite the gases with catastrophic results – the ending that all airship commanders feared most. Little wonder that the new bullets were later labelled by a reminiscing German airman as 'the invention of the devil'.

Still some miles off the English coast the L48 continued to encounter difficulties. Ellerkamm, Uecker and the other engineers had struggled for over 2 hours on the problem engines and at an altitude of 17,000ft the compass remained frozen, the weight of the airship had increased and some of the

A Farman Experimental (FE2b) fighter plane built at the Garrett Engineering Works in Leiston. This was the type of plane flown by Second Lieutenant Holder. (Taken from the *Illustrated Memorial of the Great War in relation to Leiston & District,* produced by local photographer John Smellie Waddell)

crew inside the hull had passed out with altitude sickness. Eichler and Schütze were keen to press on towards Harwich and successfully complete the raid. The silence between the men in the control car was broken only by Eichler's terse instructions to the helmsmen at the elevator and rudder wheels. In anticipation of the attack on Harwich, all lights in the control car had been extinguished and the radium coating of the instruments gave an eerie luminosity to the proceedings.

At 1.45am the L48 made landfall just south of Orfordness. At this point the engines were finally shut down for repairs and for the next 15 minutes the airship drifted helplessly over the Orfordness Experimental Station. Although the Zeppelin remained well beyond the range of both aeroplanes and anti-aircraft guns at its altitude, none of the crew could have been aware that they were hovering above an RFC airfield that had been alert and ready for action for over 3 hours.

Major Cooper and his staff on the ground heard the droning sound of the Zeppelin's engines as it approached the coast from the north-east and in the clear summer night had no difficulty in spotting the L48 as it drifted over the airfield with its engines stopped. For a few minutes they were also able to observe the passage of the L42 in the distance, travelling at much greater speed further south. At 1.48am Cooper reported the sighting to the anti-aircraft battery at Harwich. Three minutes later he telephoned the same message to Major Hargrave, Commander of the RFC's Goldhanger station in Essex, suggesting that he send up aircraft to fly north along the coast to intercept the L48.

The Orfordness station was quick to react to the sighting, sending up Second Lieutenant Clarke in a Bleriot Experimental (BE2c) aircraft at 1.50am, followed by Holder and Ashby in the FE2b at 1.55am. Conditions for the British aircraft were perfect, it being a warm summer night with excellent visibility and a large target directly overhead. Although Clarke was flying solo in the BE2c to save weight and extend the aeroplane's limited range, he was unable to climb higher than 11,000ft and after firing off a couple of drums of ammunition, out of range of the Zeppelin above, was forced to return to base. Holder and Ashby, however, continued to climb slowly at full throttle.

The Goldhanger station played host to the 37th Home Defence Squadron of the RFC. The airfield land near Wormingford, on the Blackwater Estuary, had been requisitioned in February 1917 and operated as a ground base for BE12 and FE2b fighters, tasked principally, alongside other RFC stations, with protecting the east coast from airship attacks. Patrols began soon after and continued sporadically throughout the summer of 1917, although it was not until August of that year that radio contact with the ground was established – orders to that point being communicated via ground signals. As a result air patrols were often unsuccessful in making contact with the enemy.

One of the pilots based at Goldhanger in June 1917 was the Canadian-born Second Lieutenant Loudon Pierce Watkins. 'Don' Watkins was one of four brothers, all of whom joined up and went into uniform at the outbreak of war. Alongside his brother Edward, Don went to the Toronto Curtiss School and on 7 December 1915 joined the RFC in Canada. A transfer to England followed only sixteen days later and after a period of training Watkins was confirmed as a second lieutenant on 18 May 1916. From there, he had a brief spell in France, completing a range of offensive and defensive patrols, before leaving his squadron at the end of November to take up home defence duty in England and joining the 37th Home Defence Squadron on 11 December.

Having received the telephone call from Orfordness, Major Hargrave ordered six planes to take off and patrol the coast, four from Goldhanger and two from the Rochford station in Essex. Watkins took off at 2.00am in a BE12, armed with two .303 calibre Lewis machine-guns and several drums of incendiary ammunition. The aircraft had been built by the Daimler Company of Coventry and was powered by a 150 horse-power, twelve-cylinder, air-cooled engine. As he opened up the throttle of the aircraft and climbed steadily above the station and the rural Essex countryside, Watkins scanned the heavens for the enemy dirigible. Still climbing at 8,000ft, and beginning to feel the cold chill of altitude, he then headed off in the direction of Harwich.

CHAPTER 6

Daybreak Assault

At 2.10am, having restarted its troubled engines, the L48 came inland preparing for the attack on Harwich, which Eichler, Schütze and Westphal believed to be close by. But cruising at a height of 18,400ft, the Zeppelin headed north-west for 9 miles until at 2.17am it was over the Suffolk town of Wickham Market. By this time the airship's passage was being accurately tracked and recorded by a wealth of special constables and enthusiasts – a service that would later be undertaken by the Royal Observer Corps.

On reduced power the airship meandered south from Wickham Market until it was close to the port of Felixstowe. Eichler instructed his men to prepare for action and all of the crew readied themselves for the attack. The machine-gunners in the control car stood alert and ready and the radio aerial was withdrawn, putting the airship temporarily out of contact with its ground bases back home.

All at once, and in an explosion of activity, the anti-aircraft defences at Harwich awoke. Long white fingers of light moved across the heavens, probing and feeling for the invader. With ease the searchlights found and grasped the airship, holding on firmly as it moved across the clear starlit sky. Even allowing for the control car's tinted, anti-searchlight glass, the cabin was bathed in bright light. The crew squinted, raised their hands to their eyes, moved back from the windows and prepared for the onslaught, knowing full well that the defence batteries below were about to open up.

In a pounding as severe as any of the crew had experienced before, the artillery opened up a full and sustained barrage against the height-climber. Alongside the dull and irregular booming below, reddish-yellow flames leapt from the mouths of the guns followed by the screeching dispatch of incendiary shells that crept skyward through the darkness, leaving long, deathly-white smoke trails behind them. The rain of fire

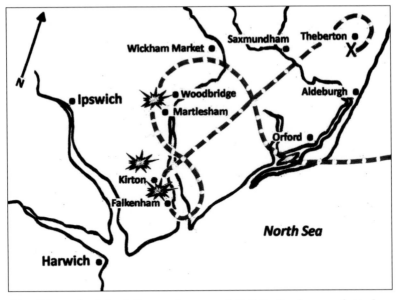

*The flight path of the L48 over the coast of Suffolk. Bombs were dropped on
Martlesham, Falkenham and Kirton.*

exploded around the airship – bright balls of light hissing and
splintering into a thousand crimson bursts of shrapnel. Shrill
shrieks followed droning hums as a cavalcade of shells was
launched with the tremendous thud of the guns. The
bombardment was so fierce that many local people believed a
sea attack or naval battle was taking place off the coast as the
pounding awakened them in their beds and peals of gunfire
rattled both doors and windows.

Executive Officer Mieth took charge of the bombing run,
using the speaking tube to communicate the order for the
bomb traps to be opened. With an eye pressed closely to the
airship's bomb-sight to the right of the rudder man and a hand
holding the bomb-release button, Mieth unleashed a series of
nine bombs on the village of Falkenham, some 5 miles north-
east of Harwich. As each bomb fell to earth the airship jolted
upwards, the duraluminium struts inside the hull creaking
under the considerable strain. The crew listened attentively for
the detonations below, each explosion briefly countering the

repeated thumping from the British defences. The L48 then turned west and north, unloading thirteen bombs on the fields around the village of Kirton, before heading further north to drop a salvo of three bombs on Martlesham close to the town of Ipswich. The time was 2.45am.

Believing that they had successfully completed the bombing run on Harwich, Eichler looked to set a course for home. At this stage the airship was flying at over 13,000ft, still being tracked by the searchlights and anti-aircraft fire along the coast. According to the reading on the compass, the Zeppelin was heading east and across the sea towards home. In reality, with the compass still malfunctioning, the vessel was heading north a short distance inland from the Suffolk shoreline. Within a few minutes, largely due to the clarity of vision that night, the error was realised, but by then valuable time had been lost. Desperate to clarify the exact position of his ship and the climatic conditions for the return journey, Eichler instructed Meier to call up the ground stations for bearings and weather reports. To add to the commander's woes, the forward engine then failed and the speed of the Zeppelin began to diminish.

Following successful calls to the ground stations, Mieth returned from the radio room with bearings and weather information. According to Nordholz there was a favourable tailwind at 11,000ft and the airship was instructed to descend from its present height. Eichler was keen to seize the opportunity, hoping that the lower altitude would unfreeze both his men and the magnetic compass and provide a significant boost to the flagging speed of the vessel – by now two of the engines had failed and the others were running at half-power.

Proceeding slowly in a north-easterly direction towards the coastal town of Leiston, some 25 miles north of Harwich, the L48 began to drift from side to side, the rudder controls having been disabled by the extreme temperatures experienced earlier. To Eichler's increasing frustration, the rudder man was struggling to keep the airship on a straight course and the hoped-for passage out over the sea was proving elusive. On the ground many thousands of local people, woken by the noise, crowded into streets and lanes, or peered from their bedroom windows, listening to the drone of the engines above and watching every move of the hapless Zeppelin that was silhouetted so clearly against the increasingly reddish tint of the new dawn. Some could hear the frenetic tapping of the airship's engineers high above as they laboured to make repairs to the failing motors.

In the 18ft-long starboard gondola Ellerkamm and Uecker were keeping a close eye on their engine hoping for no further trouble or breakdowns. They had already spent most of the night making repairs to the motor. As they did so, Heinrich Ahrens, a 37-year-old stoker petty officer from Bremerhaven, climbed down the ladder into the car on one of his regular maintenance rounds. Greeting them with a broad smile, Ahrens beckoned to Ellerkamm and over the noise of the Maybach shouted into the engineer's ear, 'Hello! We've just had a wireless message to say that there's a south-west wind blowing at 11,000ft which will push us along nicely!' Ellerkamm grinned and nodded his approval before watching Ahrens climb back up into the hull, little knowing that this would be the last time he would ever see his colleague.

Struck suddenly by the darkness and lack of noise outside the airship, Ellerkamm glanced instinctively out of a window of the engine car. The artillery fire and searchlights had stopped. He recognised that this could mean only one thing – the English were sending up their aeroplanes.

Following their take-off from Orfordness, Holder and Ashby had had few problems spotting the L48 and keeping it under observation. But as a two-seater with a full load of fuel, the aircraft had climbed painfully slowly, even at full throttle. It took over half an hour for the plane to reach 10,000ft, still way below the German airship and some way off its own height ceiling. With its nose up, Holder had kept the aircraft in a steep ascent, spiralling slowly up and over the darkened rural landscape below. He had hoped that the Zeppelin would remain over its target long enough for the plane to make contact.

As they ascended, the airmen had watched a perfect tornado of shells being sent up towards the airship by the ground

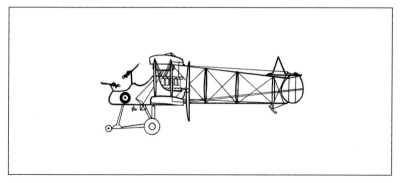

The FE2b was powered by a 160 horse-power, six-cylinder, water-cooled Beardmore engine.

batteries and their angry, flaming guns. The sky had been awash with colour from the exploding shells and the searchlights that had gripped and illuminated the besieged raider. They had heard the pounding of the British guns and the rumbling explosions that followed the Zeppelin's bomb run. And still they had continued to climb in pursuit of the L48. Having finally reached their height ceiling of around 13,000ft on the altimeter, Holder had found that the airship was still out of range but it was beginning to lose height as it headed north towards Leiston, just inside the coastline near Aldeburgh.

In his BE12 Second Lieutenant Watkins was at 11,000ft over Harwich when he saw the anti-aircraft guns begin to fire and several searchlights rise up to greet the L48. A minute later, as he pulled back the control stick to ascend, he saw the airship pass about 2,000ft above him. He climbed a further 500ft and fired one drum into the stern of the Zeppelin without effect. At 12,000ft he fired a second drum into the rear of the craft, again producing no discernible result. Recognising that he was still some way off the rapidly approaching target, he decided to wait until he was at close range before launching another attack.

For the second time that evening Major Cooper at Orfordness had sighted the L48 cruising towards his RFC station. This was at 2.45am, with the airship heading north

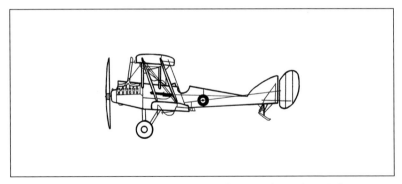

The BE12, built by the Daimler Company of Coventry, boasted a 150 horse-power, twelve-cylinder, air-cooled engine.

along the coast at an altitude lower than before, its engines droning in the awakening dawn sky. Cooper had immediately transmitted this information to the other coastal stations, fearing that Holder and Ashby had lost touch with the airship. He also instructed Captain Saundby to take off in the DH2 to challenge the raider, equipped with a .303 calibre Lewis machine-gun and five drums of mixed ammunition.

Saundby took off from Orfordness at 2.55am, by which time the Zeppelin was hovering above the station, drifting in all directions and appearing to lose height. He was pleased that he had talked Major Cooper into letting him go up on the basis of his significant experience of flying the de Havilland aircraft. While the DH2 had no lights or cockpit instruments for flying in the dark, it was carrying enough fuel to last until daybreak – which was fast approaching.

The DH2 had been built by the Aircraft Manufacturing Company of Hendon, near London. Similar aircraft had arrived in France for service less than a year before. Given an endurance capability of around 3 hours and a height ceiling of around 13,000ft, the plane had proved to be both useful and popular. As he headed skyward, Saundby handled the controls of the single-seater biplane sensitively. With its overall length of just over 35ft and a wingspan some 3ft longer, he knew that the aircraft needed to be handled with care. The responsiveness and manoeuvrability of the plane made it ideal for aerial

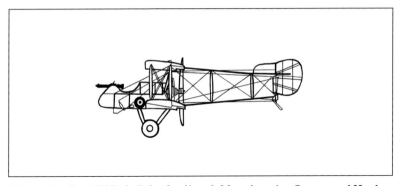

The de Havilland DH2, built by the Aircraft Manufacturing Company of Hendon, had a Monosoupape rotary engine.

combat and aerobatics, although over-handling could just as easily throw the craft into a spin. In one such incident, a DH2 had caught fire, earning it the unwelcome nickname 'the spinning incinerator'.

Saundby kept the plane's Monosoupape rotary engine at full throttle as he ascended quickly. At 3.05am the aircraft was observed to be climbing steadily above the Aldeburgh to Saxmundham railway line. With the excellent forward visibility of the DH2, Saundby had watched the L48 heading north-east from the direction of Felixstowe. Five minutes later, while still climbing at full speed, he began firing towards the stern of the airship, dispatching a couple of drums of Pomeroy ammunition and tracer but failing to make any impression on the stricken Zeppelin. He could see that the L48 was losing height, but without dashboard lights he could not read the altimeter of the DH2. He continued to climb rapidly towards the tail of the airship.

Further south, Dietrich's L42 had by this time carried out a very successful attack, striking a Royal Navy ammunition store and causing heavy damage. The airship had hovered above its target for no more than 15 minutes and its bombing run had lasted only a few moments. Despite this, it had proved to be decisive. Dietrich later commented that, 'A whole squadron of airships has been sent out merely to do two minutes' work ...'. However, what the crew believed to be

A machine-gun platform on the L42. This airship carried out a successful raid on Ramsgate on the night of 16 June 1917.

Dover was in fact Ramsgate and the attack had left three civilians dead and a further fourteen injured. Despite the operation of the anti-aircraft guns and fourteen searchlights below, the L42 had remained unseen at its altitude, largely due to the black dope on its envelope, and had slipped away from Ramsgate unchallenged. With its engines at full speed, the airship's commanders had given up any thought of attacking London and the L42 was now heading north-north-west on the homeward leg of its raid, some 70 miles away from the L48. In pursuit were three aircraft from the RFC base at Great Yarmouth that had taken off alongside nine others from the coastal station.

As the long pale streaks of the new day emerged through the dawn, the L48 passed over the town of Leiston and headed towards the tiny village of Theberton, still crippled by its failing engines and damaged rudder. The sky was a vibrant pearly grey, splashed with tinges of lavender and crimson. It was 3.15am and the anti-aircraft guns had fallen ominously silent.

Still descending, the airship was now at 12,000ft and facing east, with Commander Eichler desperate to pick up the promised tailwind. In a concerted attack the three RFC planes flown by Holder, Watkins and Saundby besieged the L48. From the ground, the hovering airship and the swarm of hornets attacking it from every quarter transfixed the many thousands of onlookers. At short intervals they heard the rapid firing of the machine-guns and saw the tiny flicker of green-sparking flames from the incendiary bullets and the red and green sidelights of two of the three planes.

Flying from north to south, and attacking the bow of the airship without any illumination, Saundby was now less than 1,000ft below the dirigible. He raised his machine-gun to an angle of 45 degrees and began firing off a double-drum of incendiary ammunition towards the nose of the Zeppelin. All at once, alerted by his tracer bullets, the gunners on the L48 returned a volley of fire with their heavy, slow-firing Maxim machine-gun. Saundby kept his nerve, firing off the full double-drum before manoeuvring the DH2 out of the way of the enemy fire. As he did so, he could see another aircraft flying above him and north-west of the airship.

With the continuing descent of the raider, Holder and Ashby now found the Zeppelin well within their range. Holder opened fire from the FE2b, but his Lewis gun jammed. He then altered course, attacking the L48 from the starboard rear, to provide Ashby with a better aim. The section sergeant began firing three drums into the airship from a range of about 300 yards, during which both airmen could see tracer bullets coming from the opposite direction.

For his part Watkins was now 500ft below the airship, still climbing, and attacking the rear of the craft from the port side. It was his tracer fire that Holder and Ashby could see. As he began firing his last drum of ammunition, he could see Saundby's plane flying across the bow of the Zeppelin.

The simultaneous attack proved too much for the stricken airship. Gas cells in both the forward and rear sections of the hull were punctured and ignited by the mixed ammunition. As

Holder began to take evasive action to avoid Watkins' tracer fire, he saw flames appearing at the Zeppelin's starboard rear. Watkins watched as the fire began to run along both sides of the hull. Saundby saw black smoke emerging from the nose of the craft, followed by a loud explosion that rocked the enemy airship. Within seconds the whole structure was enveloped in flames and falling to earth, the weight of the engines in the rear gondola dragging the burning ship down at an angle of 60 degrees, leaving a long trail of black smoke in the dawn sky. The time was 3.25am.

The British attack had taken the airship crew by surprise. In the starboard engine car Heinz Ellerkamm believed that they were over the sea and on their way home. He had elected to check the fuel supply to the engine and had shouted across to Uecker, 'Take charge here for a moment or two, I'm going to have a look at the petrol.' He had then begun to climb up the ladder into the hull in his heavy overcoat and large felt overshoes, the chill and thinness of the air outside the car making him gasp. As he reached the middle of the ladder he had heard the faint rattle of machine-gun fire in the distance, and then heard another sustained volley as he stepped on to the lateral gangway inside the hull. Terrified, he had watched as flaming phosphorous bullets began to tear at the gas cells in the rear of the airship.

Inside the hull Ellerkamm could see tiny blue flames coming from the rear fifth and sixth gas cells. He then heard a dull explosion, similar to the noise made when a gas stove is lit, and watched in horror as a ball of flame blasted rapidly down the length of the ship, one gas cell after another igniting angrily above his head. In the ensuing mayhem he saw the rigger running along the catwalk towards the control car. Ellerkamm had then climbed on to one of the integral girders along the side gangway, his knee pressed against a bracing wire and intense flames already clawing at his fur overcoat.

At the point of attack, Otto Mieth had just returned to the front of the control car after calling up the ground stations for weather reports and having dispatched a message to Nordholz with news of the successful raid. As he discussed the latest wind measurements from Bruges with Eichler, a bright light had illuminated the cabin. Mieth had imagined this to be a searchlight from an enemy warship, but as he looked upwards he was shocked to see that the airship was on fire. Flickering red and orange flames had begun to attack the exposed skeleton of the airship and the heat above their heads was tremendous.

Stunned now by the drama unfolding around him, Mieth heard Schütze shout out, 'The ship is crashing in flames!' Mieth threw off his overcoat, shouting for the others to do the same. He feared that if the airship crashed into the sea they would be drowned by the weight of their heavy fur garments. But Schütze and Eichler were motionless, realising that the airship was doomed and there was very little chance of survival for the crew. This was their constant nightmare, to be burned alive in an airship crashing to earth over enemy territory – an event from which there had been no survivors in the history of German aerial warfare. But Schütze stood still, resolute and unwavering, staring defiantly at the flames above. Around him, equally static at their posts, stood other members of the crew, each making no sound as the Zeppelin began to fall earthwards like a flaming comet. Then, as if bidding Mieth farewell, Schütze turned and announced above the roar of the flames, 'It's all over'.

Still flying beneath the ill-fated Zeppelin and awestruck by the speed of its destruction, Saundby watched as the vessel collapsed into a 'V' shape, falling slowly away from his plane. The noise of the blaze was so loud that it drowned out the sound of his rotary engine. Holder and Ashby also watched the descent of the airship, circling the Zeppelin as it fell to earth. Holder's emotions were a mixture of exhilaration and sorrow as he witnessed the terrible ordeal of the German crew. He felt no bitterness towards them, recognising, as a fellow airman, their commitment to duty and the appalling risks they faced.

The catastrophic descent took about 7 minutes, the air whistling through the craft as it dropped, fanning the flames to the port side. A tall column of fire rose from the stricken craft for many hundreds of feet, illuminating the sky like a second sun and hungrily consuming the $1,970,800ft^3$ of hydrogen gas. Ellerkamm continued to cling to the struts along the walkway, the strong rush of air driving the flames away from him. But the intensity of the heat still seared the exposed areas of his skin and charred his over garments. As he tried to beat out the flames on his fur coat his sleeve caught fire. He wondered if he should jump, remembering Schütze's one-time pronouncement at Nordholz that it would be 'better to smash against the earth and perish at once than to burn to death trapped in blazing wreckage on the ground'. He decided to stay where he was, gripping desperately on to the disintegrating structure around him, thinking of home and his fiancée Gretel, and wondering whether this was his time to die.

Lieutenant Mieth was in no mood to die. Having worked his way from the front of the control car to the radio room, he leapt towards the side window intent on jumping. But as he did so, the burning frame of the airship groaned and creaked, collapsing noisily around him and snapping strut after strut in rapid succession. The forward gondola swayed backwards and away from the inferno, throwing Mieth into a corner and flinging Meier the wireless operator on top of him. The car began to grind against the skeleton of the airship as gas and flames flared over the crewmen. Mieth could feel the scorching heat on his face and was aware of groans from his colleague. He covered his head with his arms, hoping for a release from the pain and passed slowly away into another world.

The other crew members who had not already perished hung on where they could, a few choosing to leap from the craft rather than face death by burning. One of these was Schütze himself, who leapt from the control car as it began to disintegrate around him, jumping earthwards just before the airship crashed. Further back, in his starboard gondola, Wilhelm Uecker braced himself for the crash.

A little after 3.30am on 17 June 1917 the flaming hulk of the L48 passed over Holly Tree Farm on the outskirts of Theberton. One of its remaining fuel tanks fell away from the craft, exploding loudly as it hit the ground, blasting a large crater and shooting tall flames high up into the sky above the sleepy village. The remainder of the giant airship made contact with a tremendous bumping and grinding of metal, one half coming to rest on cultivated land, the other across a ploughed field. The wild conflagration continued unabated, the glow visible for many miles across the Suffolk landscape. In the morning sky a long trail of acrid smoke traced out the path of the airship's descent and large blackened flakes of the outer covering of the vessel floated down across the fields and villages nearby.

Crossing the North Sea on its return flight, the L42 had managed to evade its pursuers despite being raked with incendiary fire and plagued by engine problems. A layer of mist had aided its escape. But as the crew of twenty reflected on their continuing good luck, a number had seen the silhouette of their sister-ship many miles away, hovering above the coast, in the clear sky of the early morning. As one of the attacking British planes appeared to rise above the airship, the L48 had become a bright red ball of flame.

With faces as pale as death the horrified airmen of the L42 had watched the stern of the burning airship dip before falling down through the sky amid a veritable firestorm. In silence they looked on as the dirigible fell earthwards, Dietrich imagining that through his binoculars he had seen a number of colleagues jumping from the burning Zeppelin. As he later reflected, 'Better to be broken to pieces than burnt to death.' Shortly after, they had radioed the news of the loss through to Nordholz.

Against this grim backdrop they had travelled home for many more hours, remaining at over 13,000ft for most of the journey, landing at Nordholz at 9.10am. Many of the crew had suffered from the effects of prolonged altitude sickness. As the L42 put down, Peter Strasser was the first to climb aboard, eager for details of the crash and unwilling to accept that the height-climber had been brought down by enemy aircraft. 'The English have no real defence against our airships!' he insisted. But Dietrich would not be browbeaten. 'It was a plane!' he retorted, 'I saw it myself!' Strasser left the control car weary and despondent, spending most of the next few days alone in his quarters. He was not sure whether the Naval Airship Division could continue to withstand such heavy and tragic losses.

CHAPTER 7

Burials and Benevolence

With the shock of the crash Otto Mieth was jolted momentarily back into the real world. In terror he awoke to a continuing scene of collapsing debris, scorching metal and red-hot bracing wires. Choking heat and smoke filled what remained of the radio cabin, burning his lungs, and for the second time Mieth slipped back into unconsciousness. But luck was on his side.

As the immense frame of the airship had approached the ground, the control car had collided with a tall tree, the impact wrenching it up and away from the blistering flames of the burning ship, and thus saving Mieth from certain death. Wilhelm Meier had not been so fortunate – the force of the impact had broken his back.

Heinz Ellerkamm had also continued his run of good luck. After the initial din of the crash he found himself amid a burning maze of girders, wires, struts and fittings. His overcoat was still smouldering and behind him he could see a river of liquid fire. Some of his muscles had been torn and he was finding it difficult to breathe, the wind having been knocked out of him. He kept reminding himself that he had survived – a thought that gave him added strength. Ahead of him he could see a glimmer of light. As he concentrated his efforts on pushing away the girder in front of him, another gave way opening up a small gap. He crawled forward breathing in short gasps and managed to break free of the tangled wreckage. Beneath his burnt hands he felt wet grass and smelt fresh air. It was now almost full daylight.

Out in the open air, but still only feet away from the burning craft, Ellerkamm rolled over in the grass and collapsed exhausted. In the bright sunlit rays of the early morning he squinted and, as his eyes became accustomed to the brightness, saw that he now lay in a picturesque English meadow. Some horses were running around uncontrollably

Some of the headlines in the national and local press reporting the destruction of the L48.

with their tails in the air and as he struggled to take in the surreal nature of the scene around him a wild duck flew overhead. He then heard the drone of an aeroplane circling above the crash site and glanced up at the British plane, astonished to see the pilot waving at him.

Frank Holder and Sydney Ashby had followed the airship down to earth in their FE2b and had continued circling the wreckage looking for survivors. Holder was thrilled to see Ellerkamm emerge from the debris, convinced that all of the crew had perished. Out of respect for his fellow airman he smiled and waved at Ellerkamm before flying off to land back at Orfordness at 4.05am. Robert Saundby had landed his DH2 at the station 15 minutes earlier and Loudon Watkins had safely flown the 35 miles back to the Goldhanger station at Wormingford, landing at 4.03am. Saundby was later to record the incident in his operational log-book, writing simply, 'Night flight after Zeps – during which Holder and I brought one down in flames near Middleton [*sic*].'

Mr H. Staulkey, a local farmer, owned Holly Tree Farm. He and his wife had been awakened in the early hours of the morning by the noise of the firing and the exploding fuel tank of the L48. In a state of some alarm, both had watched from their bedroom window as the blazing hulk of the Zeppelin passed by and crashed to earth in one of their fields less than a quarter of a mile away. The explosions had continued around the crash site alongside the terrific firestorm, the blaze continuing for at least an hour.

Both dressed quickly, Staulkey pulling on his working clothes and donning a jacket, hat, boots and leggings before setting off across the fields. His wife was traumatised and too afraid to leave the house to attend the crash site. Over the coming hours she kept herself busy entertaining the numerous visitors to the farmhouse and providing well water for the many thirsty cyclists.

The L48 was a pitiful sight. The enormous frame of the airship was broken in two, the tail section a mass of indistinguishable twisted metal. About 80ft of its nose end rose up obliquely into the air pointing south, gleaming in the sunshine. One of the large Maybach engines could be seen, buried vertically into the ground. Shreds of envelope material clung to the skeleton and fluttered gently in the breeze. The remains of the control car, other than the radio room that was still hung up in a tree, lay to the side of the wreck, the dead body of one of the crew still clearly visible. And all around fires were smouldering, keen flames breaking out every so often as another pool of petrol ignited in the aftermath.

Across the site there were large, blackened patches of earth where burning fuel had rained down, destroying the vegetation underneath. At intervals lay the mangled bodies of men who had leapt from the airship in its dying moments – each twisted and disfigured by the descent, limbs broken and clothes torn. On one could be seen the bright uniform buttons of the Naval Airship Division, marked *Kaiserliche Marine*.

In among the wreckage lay the charred remains of most of the crew members, including Stoker Petty Officers Wilhelm Gluckel, Michael Neunzig and Hermann von Stockum, Helmsmen Paul Hannemann and Franz Konig, Senior Sailor Paul Suchlich from Niedersalzbrunn, Sailors Karl Ploger and Wilhelm Betz and Signalling Officers Walter Dippmann and Heinrich Herbst. All had suffered the most terrible of deaths.

Near the edge of the field lay the heavy body of Corvette Captain Viktor Schütze, all alone in death. His beautifully tailored uniform was embellished with gold lace and his Iron Cross, First Class, over the top of which hung his heavy fur coat. The senior airship officer's face was bruised and his head was bent under him indicating that he had fallen to earth headfirst – an unfitting end for such a talented and dedicated airman.

With the flames still raging behind him, Ellerkamm rose to his feet and began to stagger around the crash site in a daze, desperate to find other surviving colleagues and destroy any confidential papers he could find. He passed Schütze's body, knowing that his former commander had jumped, as he always said he would.

As Ellerkamm wandered around, a man dressed in a shirt and trousers ran towards him. Chief Petty Officer F.W. Bird, who lived less than a mile away from the crash site and happened to be home on leave from the Royal Navy, stared incredulously at the German and asked, 'Are you from the Zeppelin?' Ellerkamm was confused and could not understand more than a few words. Bird began to gesticulate to make himself understood and eventually requested that the airman place his hands above his head while Bird searched him. Bird then proceeded to remove Ellerkamm's knife and purse, the

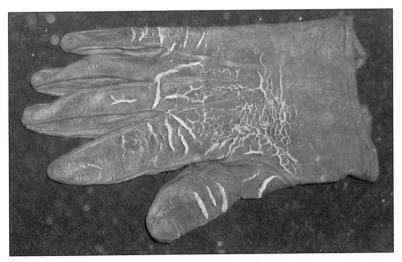

A glove belonging to one of the airship's crew, now displayed in the Leiston Long Shop Museum.

latter containing a number of German and English coins and a railway ticket.

By this stage local civilians and police were beginning to arrive, and were soon joined by the 1st and 6th Battalion of Suffolk Cyclists from Saxmundham and members of the Royal

The remains of a gondola and engine parts from the Zeppelin. (John Smellie Waddell/Frank Huxley collection)

The skeleton of the crashed airship, surrounded by sightseers. (John Smellie Waddell/Frank Huxley collection)

Army Medical Corps. One of these was Captain R. Powell of the 319th Field Ambulance Division at Yoxford. He had earlier seen the L48 in trouble and had bundled five stretcher-bearers into an ambulance before heading off to Theberton.

Powell, Bird, Ellerkamm and others helped to pull Lieutenant Mieth from the debris of the radio cabin. Astonishingly he was still alive, but was covered in burns and both his legs were broken. Powell placed him on a stretcher and then examined his injuries, bandaging his many wounds. Mieth stirred and half-raised himself from the stretcher, realising that he had broken bones and severe lacerations on his head and hands. His chest felt heavy and it was painful when he breathed. One of the Englishmen held a cigarette case under his nose in a friendly gesture and asked, 'Do you want a cigarette?' Mieth lay back down on the stretcher and passed out once more.

Many more helpers and onlookers were now arriving at the scene, including a vast number of local people who busied themselves collecting souvenirs and relics from the mangled airship. Soldiers soon placed a cordon around the skeleton of the L48 and attempted to extinguish the remaining fires.

Bird took charge of the prisoner Ellerkamm, marching him to the farmhouse where he was given a cup of tea by the

Soldiers guarding the many miles of duraluminium scattered over the crash site. (John Smellie Waddell/Frank Huxley collection)

kindly Mrs Staulkey. Ellerkamm asked to be taken to see Mieth, but was told that this was not possible. He was later escorted away by two sergeants from the army and taken under guard to Darsham railway station and then on to Ipswich. While he was there, a large crowd gathered, eager to see one of the fearsome Zeppelin bombers. As Ellerkamm stepped off the train under military escort one man made plain his views, shouting across to the German airman, 'May yer wake up in the morning and find yerself as far through hell as a hare can run in a fortnight!'

Machinist's Mate Wilhelm Uecker was pulled from the wreckage of his engine gondola by civilians, carried to a stretcher and placed under the care of Captain Powell. Powell made him as comfortable as he could and offered the airman water. Uecker had numerous burns and it was later realised that he had severe internal injuries. Before being taken away, both Uecker and Mieth were searched, the contents of their pockets being passed to some of the army officers present.

From the crew of nineteen, only Ellerkamm, Mieth and Uecker had survived. Even this was a miracle given the circumstances and severity of the crash. They became the first,

The remains of a second gondola from the L48. (John Smellie Waddell/Frank Huxley collection)

and last, German airmen to survive the crash of a burning airship over enemy territory.

The weather that summer's day continued to be hot and cloudless. Elsewhere in the world the German raider *Seeadler* captured the schooner *RC Slade* in the Pacific Ocean and 3,000 miners went on strike in Bisbee, America, over pay and

The nose of the airship as seen from one of the lanes close to the crash site. (John Smellie Waddell/Frank Huxley collection)

A section of the debris where a number of bodies were found. (John Smellie Waddell/Frank Huxley collection)

conditions. The Lone Star Corporation released the film *The Immigrant*, directed by and starring Charlie Chaplin, who on the same day signed a new film contract worth $1,075,000 a year. The day also saw the birth of Dino Paul Crocetti, later to be known as Dean Martin, the popular American singing and comedy star of the 1950s.

The remains of the airship's radiators. (John Smellie Waddell/Frank Huxley collection)

Petrol tanks and supply cans recovered from the wreckage. (John Smellie Waddell/ Frank Huxley collection)

The remainder of the day at Holly Tree Farm was busy and frenetic, with an estimated 30,000 people visiting the crash site – a staggering number given the rural nature of the area, the limitations of travel and the petrol rationing in operation for the small number of people fortunate enough to have access to a motorised vehicle.

Despite some early gains by the souvenir hunters, the military managed to swiftly erect a barbed-wire barricade around the remains of the L48 and a cordon of police officers and soldiers held back the growing crowd as people came and went all day. Twenty minutes after the barricade had been erected five bodies that had been found in nearby fields were brought within the enclosure and covered, away from the public gaze. Bill Munnings, a 13-year-old who had cycled from his home at Bramfield to be one of the first people on the scene, watched as the bodies were covered up. When he arrived, he placed his solitary bicycle against some railings. Leaving later at around 11.00am he could not even get close to his machine as it was by then covered up by some 200 other cycles.

The crash scene had more of a carnival atmosphere about it than the solemn and tragic event it really was. As the

Some of the officers who supervised the clearance, together with Farmer Staulkey. (John Smellie Waddell/Frank Huxley collection)

professionals scoured the wreckage for survivors and military intelligence against a grisly backdrop of fire, death and destruction, sightseers in festive mood arrived from near and far. A collection box passed around the crowd raised some £30 for the nearby East Suffolk & Ipswich Hospital. A local lad found half a loaf of German black bread in a field and sold bits of it to souvenir hunters, making himself 10*d* in cash and retaining a small piece for himself.

The various branches of the military worked long and hard to secure the site and recover what they could from the wreckage. Naval engineers put up a marquee for the dissection of the L48, while surveyors and draughtsmen recorded all of the details of the vessel. Three officers from Admiralty Intelligence arrived and asked for all the bodies to be searched and all personal items from the crew to be secured in bags. The detailed combing of the control car yielded a number of important papers, not the least of which were codes and cipher tables for the German Naval Signal Book – documents that the L48 should not have been carrying and which were extremely valuable to the British Navy. By the end of the month the Germans had been forced to change the compromised codes.

A tangled mess of airship parts. (John Smellie Waddell/Frank Huxley collection)

The local and national press had a field day in announcing the news of the crashed Zeppelin. The leader writer of the *Eastern Daily Press* announced, 'East Anglia has been privileged to witness over a wide area the fiery destruction of one of these gasbags with its crew of marauders ...'. The tone of the press coverage echoed the general triumphalism of the local population in witnessing the crash. For them it was another telling and visible blow to the German military campaign.

Scaffolding was brought in to shore up the nose of the craft on 18 June when thunderstorms looked likely to flatten the framework. Admiralty technicians from the Construction Department of the Pulham Air Station in Norfolk arrived on the same day and were particularly interested in the design of the Zeppelin, this being one of the newly commissioned height-climbers. Each component part was carefully measured and scrutinised, many of the lessons learnt later being put into operation on British dirigibles.

Men from the Royal Naval Air Service (RNAS) were charged with the dismantling operation under the command of Flight Lieutenant Victor Goddard. They made hundreds of journeys to the nearby goods yard at Leiston railway station

RNAS men dismantling the wreckage. (John Smellie Waddell/Frank Huxley collection)

with truckloads of duraluminium which were finally taken away by rail. By Tuesday, 19 June they had also recovered the bodies of fourteen of the sixteen crew members who had perished.

The nose of the airship prior to its departure from the site. (John Smellie Waddell/Frank Huxley collection)

The nose of the airship being loaded for transportation. (John Smellie Waddell/ Frank Huxley collection)

The weather was again hot and bright on the morning of Wednesday, 20 June. An inquest chaired by Ipswich Coroner Bernard Petty was held in the front garden of Staulkey's farmhouse and revealed that of the fourteen bodies recovered, five had died from injuries consistent with falling to earth and the remainder had been burnt to death. Only four of the crew had been formally identified as a result of documents found on them. The coroner and jury returned a verdict consistent with the medical evidence.

During the afternoon the burial of the fourteen airmen took place in the churchyard of St Peter's in Theberton, with many hundreds of local people lining the route. Frank Garrett, the manager of the nearby Garrett Engineering Works (now the site of the Leiston Long Shop Museum), allowed a number of women from the munitions department of the factory to dig the graves for the airmen. The location was incongruous given the essential Englishness of the church, with its thick stone walls and preserved Norman masonry, its gargoyles and altar tomb, and the finely carved stone niche above the old church doorway. This church was reputed to have had associations with smuggling, one of the most enduring of English coastal

The tail end of the airship which survived the crash largely intact. (John Smellie Waddell/Frank Huxley collection)

Truckloads of duraluminium from the crash site were taken away by rail via Leiston station. (John Smellie Waddell/Frank Huxley collection)

crimes, as far back as 1747. The bodies of these brave German airmen were indeed a long way from home.

The ceremony itself was well orchestrated and straightforward. The coffins were transported from Holly Tree Farm on gun carriages and army wagons, in convoy with an

The coroner and inquest jury. (John Smellie Waddell/Frank Huxley collection)

St Peter's Church, Theberton, where the crew of the L48 were buried for forty-nine years.

A team of women from the munitions department of the Garrett Engineering Works in Leiston volunteered to dig the graves for the Zeppelin airmen. (Long Shop Project Trust)

officer and a squad from one of the cyclist battalions. In the churchyard men from the RFC and RNAS, an army chaplain, the local rector, a Roman Catholic priest and hundreds of onlookers greeted the cortège in silence as the sun continued to cast a warm glow over the proceedings. Not a single shot was fired and a simple burial service was read before each coffin was lowered into a solitary grave. A wreath placed on top of Commander Eichler's coffin read, 'To a very brave enemy from RFC officers'. Placing such wreaths was common practice in France, where flying officers had a high degree of respect for their German counterparts, but here it was to meet with some criticism locally. In a further act of benevolence, one of the onlookers placed some flowers on the grave. The message with them said they were from an Englishman, 'who understands that each of these souls is somebody's son'.

During the next two days the remains of the L48 were further cleared, enabling the recovery of the bodies of the final two crewmen, one of whom was identified as Karl Milich, a 36-year-old stoker petty officer born in Striegau. Both bodies were buried in the churchyard alongside their colleagues.

The clear-up operation was to take nearly two months, the wreckage of the L48 lying for weeks where it fell, visited daily

The coffin of Commander Eichler being carried by officers of the RFC. (John Smellie Waddell/Frank Huxley collection)

The original gravestones in Theberton Church. The bodies of the crew were eventually moved to a national cemetery for German war dead in Staffordshire. (John Waddell collection)

by hundreds of sightseers. Throughout the period what had become known locally as the 'Zeppelin field' was guarded by dozens of soldiers, although small amounts of pillaging continued unchecked.

The graves of the crew would remain at Theberton for the next forty-nine years. A sign paid for by the RFC contained an inscription from *Romans* (14:4) which read, 'Who art thou that judgest another man's servant? To his own master he standeth or falleth.' The site was also adorned with simple stone memorial tablets that were sent over from Germany, travelling by sea to Southampton, by train to Leiston and by horse to Theberton, the work being organised by James Coates, landlord of the nearby Red Lion public house.

Ellerkamm, Mieth and Uecker were not given the opportunity to attend the funeral of their colleagues, although the latter two were, in any case, in no fit state to attend such a ceremony. Mieth had come round on the morning after the day of the crash to find that he was in a clean bed in an English field hospital. With most local hospitals overrun with wounded servicemen from the Western Front, Mieth was transported to

A remembrance plaque erected in the churchyard of St Peter's and paid for by officers from the RFC.

the Ranelagh Road School in Ipswich, which had been requisitioned and temporarily converted into a field hospital. Despite the fears of some of the nursing staff that Mieth would be unwelcome among the British walking wounded, his good nature and character were such that when he left the hospital, to be taken to a prisoner of war camp, many of the staff and patients assembled to bid him farewell.

During his stay at Ranelagh Mieth also came under the scrutiny of British Military Intelligence. An undercover MI5 colonel, posing as a German prisoner with shell shock, was placed in a bed in the same room as Mieth. Over time the colonel built up such a rapport with the German airman that Mieth was convinced the agent was a fellow German. However, despite the subterfuge, Mieth appeared to have no useful information to offer beyond the view that his nation had started the war and would almost certainly lose it. After ten days the colonel was moved from Ranelagh. Mieth was to survive not only this war, but the next as well, eventually passing away on 30 April 1956 at Iranga, Tanganyika. His own account of the demise of the L48 was published in 1926.

Ellerkamm also continued his run of good luck, although not without some heartache. He was taken to a prisoner of war camp where he was interrogated. Like Mieth he had no useful information to offer. Sadly, his parents and fiancée received news that he had died in the crash and it was some weeks later before he was able to get word to them that he was in fact still alive. It would also be some years later before he learnt that Mieth had survived the crash and the war. The hard-working Ellerkamm later became landlord of a pub on the corner of Schlachterstrasse, near St Michael's Church in Hamburg. He died on 4 August 1963 at Heidelberg. His crash adventures were also published in a book after the war, alongside the colourful stories of other surviving members of the Naval Airship Division. Recounting the crash, he remained convinced that it was the radio message from the German ground station – advising the airship to descend to 11,000ft in order to catch a favourable tailwind – which had brought the L48 within the range of enemy fire and ultimately caused its downfall. Having escaped with only superficial burns, he commented that it had not been his time to die.

Uecker was not so fortunate. Having survived the crash, he struggled against a variety of internal injuries and illnesses, including a burst bladder, and eventually died in England on 11 November 1918 – the last day of the war.

For the British airmen the aftermath of the incident was no less convoluted, with many conflicting accounts of the facts surrounding the destruction of the L48. Two weeks after the crash the War Office announced that His Majesty the King had conferred the Military Cross for conspicuous gallantry on Captain Robert Saundby and Second Lieutenant Loudon Watkins. On 7 August a further announcement was made that the King had approved the Military Cross and Military Medal respectively for Second Lieutenant Frank Holder and Sergeant Sydney Ashby.

Saundby survived the war and resigned his Territorial Force Commission on 1 August 1919, continuing his career in the Royal Air Force (RAF) and later the Air Ministry. On 21

January 1926 he was awarded the Distinguished Flying Cross and was appointed Commander in Chief of Bomber Command in 1943. The following year he was knighted and later promoted to the post of air marshal. After a long and successful military and writing career, Saundby died in 1971 at his home in Burghclere, Berkshire.

Watkins was promoted to temporary captain and flight commander on 8 August 1917, later being posted to France as part of 148 Squadron. By the early part of May 1918 the squadron was based at Sains Les Pernes and engaged in operations to bomb enemy aerodromes, billets and rail junctions. On 1 July, while flying a night-bombing mission, he crashed and died in a FE2d plane near Ostreville, although his observer survived. The official casualty report blamed an engine failure for the crash, a broken rocker arm on one of the engine's cylinders being cited as the most likely cause.

A few weeks after the destruction of the L48, Holder survived a plane crash at the village of Eastbridge, next to Theberton. He remained at the Orfordness station until the summer of 1919. After resigning his commission at the end of the war, he became deputy mayor and an alderman of Chelmsford Town Council and received the Order of the British Empire. He also served in the RAF during the Second World War and later became a Justice of the Peace. He died on 17 October 1978 at his home in Danbury, Essex.

Like Watkins, Ashby would not see life beyond the war. Only weeks after Holder's crash at Eastbridge, Ashby died in a plane crash at Martlesham in Suffolk.

For years after the war a local man tended the burial site of the L48's crew, trimming the grass every two weeks and placing fresh wild flowers on the graves. It was said locally that he had served in France and had been one of only two survivors from a company of forty men sent into battle. On Armistice Day every year he stood silently by the graves of the German crewmen for two minutes. But he was not the only person to continue the show of goodwill – on the night of 16 June each year an unknown woman placed a wreath on the graves.

In 1964 a site was chosen in England as a national cemetery for German war dead. The Cannock Chase cemetery, once a royal hunting forest and in Tudor times a source of fuel for the iron industry, was chosen because its pine-covered slopes looked similar to parts of Germany. The cemetery became the final resting place for all German servicemen who died in Britain during the two world wars. The bodies of the crew of the L48 were moved there in 1966, along with other fallen Zeppelin crews, and buried in a grave under four large slabs to the side of the entrance vestibule. A plaque above the grave in English and German reads, 'Side by side with their comrades, the crews of four Zeppelins shot down over England during the First World War, here found their resting place. The fallen were brought here from their original burial places at Potters Bar, Great Burstead and Theberton. The members of each crew are buried in caskets in one grave.' Each crew member is commemorated by name and rank.

These 6 acres of Staffordshire stand as a lasting reminder of the many hundreds of servicemen who died fighting for their country on or above foreign lands and seas. With its surrounding birch and pine trees, spring daffodils and summer heather, the cemetery is a fitting tribute to the bravery and dedication of the airshipmen of the L48.

CHAPTER 8

Epilogue – Photographs, Fragments and Folklore

The crash of the L48 has become an endearing and enduring part of Suffolk folklore, where myth, reality, fact and fiction have combined in the minds of the many thousands of people who either witnessed or remembered the event or had the story passed down to them by those who claimed to. With the passage of years the incident has also prompted regular local press and media features, each supported by a wide variety of colourful, and sometimes wholly inaccurate, first-hand accounts of the crash and its after-effects. The Zeppelin field lives on in the minds of many, although few could now locate it with ease.

And yet the destruction of the L48 was tragic, tangible and real. On the mantelpieces of many a Suffolk home, above the bars of certain public houses, in the exhibitions of a few local museums and in the porch of St Peter's Church in Theberton can be found some of the physical remnants. From preserved aluminium struts and girders to fashioned trinkets, ashtrays and oddities, the relics turn up with alarming frequency – testament perhaps to the success of the thieves, looters and souvenir hunters that preyed upon the carcass of the fatally wounded airship.

But the story of the destruction also lives on as a result of two sets of photographs taken opportunistically and independently of each other at the time of the crash. The first was a set of aerial shots, detailing the full extent of the crash site, the devastation and the security arrangements, taken by Captain W. Walter Hammond, a photographic officer from the Orfordness station. Hammond, a good friend of Frank Holder, was taken up in the pilot's FE2b on the morning of 17 June, circling the smoking wreck of the airship and photographing the complete scene. Local Leiston photographer J.S. Waddell,

Wreckage from the L48 in the porch of St Peter's Church, Theberton.

of the Hayling Studio, took the second batch, a comprehensive and illuminating series of shots covering the full diary of events from the crash through to the burial of the crew. His subsequent, published, photographic booklet has become the definitive visual record of the incident and a lasting reminder of the remarkable events that occurred that summer.

At the time, in an age before global and up-to-the-minute news coverage, the event pushed the small community of Theberton into the limelight and the national press, although most official reports left out the name of the village for security reasons. But there was a more chilling subtext to this media attention – the shooting down of the Zeppelin was a

Sections of duraluminium girders in the Leiston Long Shop Museum.

visible, lasting and devastating demonstration that no part of Britain, not even the sleepy, out of the way villages and towns of rural Suffolk, would ever again be immune to the ravages of total war.

The destruction of the L48 was a very telling indication that in the battle for wartime air supremacy, it was the aeroplane

Examples of the souvenirs made from the wreckage of the L48. (John Smellie Waddell/Frank Huxley collection)

A modern reminder of the L48's history: an ashtray fashioned from part of the wreckage of the airship.

This booklet, produced by Leiston photographer John Smellie Waddell, has become the definitive visual record of the L48 crash.

that was now in the ascendancy. A Zeppelin commander who survived the war claimed, 'It was not the guns of the enemy that drove us from the North Sea, or rather ever higher and higher in mid-air, but the enemy aeroplanes.' But while Britain could draw some comfort from the fact that its home defence squadrons now stood a reasonable chance of bringing down a Zeppelin, and the volume of airship raids began to decrease significantly, the threat of attack continued with the start of bombing by long-range Gotha and Giant aeroplanes in the summer of 1917.

Later that year Germany began to divert scarce aluminium and rubber resources from airship to aeroplane production. Its bombers began to attack London and other targets with increasing success. Even for strategic scouting operations across the North Sea, the aeroplane was fast becoming preferable to the airship. Count Zeppelin himself had announced earlier in the year that 'airships are an antiquated weapon. The aeroplane will control the air.' During 1916 his organisation had already moved into aeroplane construction.

And yet the end of the war did not bring an end to the Zeppelin airship industry or indeed lessen the strong faith in the potential of dirigibles which, with the benefits of significant technological advances, has continued to the present day. For Germany in the immediate post-war period it was the resurgence of interest in commercial airship travel that sustained the investment in Zeppelins.

Having won the war, the Allies sought to dismantle Germany's military capacity. This included the once thriving airship construction industry. Those airships which were not destroyed by their ever-loyal crews on 23 June 1919 were distributed among the European nations as war reparations. Beyond this, the severity of the terms of the Treaty of Versailles and the precarious financial situation in Germany did little to increase business confidence in the surviving Zeppelin Company. Under the treaty, Germany was prohibited from building any further military airships.

In the event it was the USA that did most to ensure that the Zeppelin name lived on in the early 1920s. As a non-signatory to the Treaty of Versailles, the United States had not benefited from the redistribution of German airships as war reparations. Its military chiefs could see a future for Zeppelin-type airships and were keen to work with the company in building a suitable aircraft for American use. Using its diplomatic strength, the USA convinced a conference of ambassadors on 16 December 1921 to allow such an airship to be built at Friedrichshafen, the completed airship later being flown to the United States in October 1924 and renamed the USS *Los Angeles*. The USA was also instrumental in negotiating the 1925 Treaty of Locarno which lifted the remaining Allied restrictions on the building of airships in Germany.

The period beyond this saw a renaissance in the prestige and fortunes of the Zeppelin Company as it developed its commercial airship capabilities with the construction of the *Graf Zeppelin* and *Hindenburg*. The *Graf Zeppelin* flew for the first time on 18 September 1928. With a length of 776ft and a gas capacity of 2,650,000ft^3, it was the largest airship ever constructed. In an operating career lasting over ten years, the airship was to make 590 flights, covering over a million miles and carrying over 13,000 passengers. This included an historic 'round the world' flight during 1929 with no major delays or technical problems.

Sadly the success story of the revitalised Zeppelin Company was to be short-lived following the destruction of the *Graf Zeppelin*'s sister-ship, the *Hindenburg*. Launched in 1936, the airship had flown sixty-three times before being destroyed by fire while landing at the Lakehurst Naval Air Station in Manchester, New Jersey, on 6 May 1937. One third of those on board perished in the accident in the full glare of the American media which had turned out for the arrival of the Zeppelin flagship.

Despite the hopes of many Germans, including some in the military command, the arrival and use of airships for aerial bombing did not produce widespread devastation throughout Britain or scare the nation into submission. *The Times* on 13 January 1919 reported that German air raids between 1915 and 1918 had resulted in the deaths of 498 civilians and 58 soldiers, and injuries to a further 1,913 people – in contrast, during October 1918 some 2,225 people in London died of influenza in one week alone. The nearly 200 tons of bombs dropped during raids on England had caused damage estimated at just over £1.5 million, some £850,000 of which was in the London area. While no one could doubt that aerial bombardment had been a powerful psychological weapon, playing on the fears and anxieties of the nation's population, there was little evidence that this had led to any widespread calls for capitulation. For many, the raids had served to stiffen their opposition to what was viewed as German aggression.

And yet, as the Leader of Airships Peter Strasser declared, 'If the English should succeed in convincing us that the airship attacks had little value, and thereby cause us to give them up, they would be rid of a severe problem, and would be laughing at us in triumph behind our backs.' Like others, Strasser knew that the real value of the airship attacks lay in their capacity to tie up valuable defence personnel on the home front and to divert resources away from other theatres of war. The *British*

Official History, produced after the war, reported that by the end of 1916 British home defences consisted of 17,341 officers and men and twelve RFC squadrons, made up of some 200 officers, 2,000 men and 110 aeroplanes. All of these could otherwise have been mobilised for war overseas.

But there were costs to the Germans, too. The navy lost twenty-three airships through enemy action, with a further thirty-one being lost in accidents, explosions and lightning strikes. The Naval Airship Division also lost 74 airship officers, 264 non-commissioned officers and 50 men, or some 40 per cent of its operational personnel – many of whom might have survived had pack-parachutes been more readily available and more widely carried. Of the army's fifty airships, seventeen were destroyed by enemy fire, while others were decommissioned before the end of the war. The monetary value of these losses can only be guessed at.

In perhaps the greatest irony of the Zeppelin war story, it would be Strasser himself who would pay the ultimate price as chief promoter and supporter of the airship bombing campaign. On 5 August 1918, while commanding a raid of five Zeppelins aboard the airship L70, he was to die alongside twenty-two crewmen when his vessel was shot down by British planes just off the East Anglian coast. The L70 was a triumph of airship technology – the largest, fastest and most impressive of all Zeppelins, with seven high-altitude Maybach engines and a top speed of 81mph. While it was characteristic of Strasser's consistent approach to leading his men from the front, the event also demonstrated some of the over-confidence displayed by the Leader of Airships throughout the war. Approaching the enemy coast at around 17,000ft, Strasser wrongly believed that the L70 was beyond the reach of the British fighters called to intercept the raider. The attacking DH4 aircraft were able to close in on the airship and fire numerous rounds of explosive ammunition into its hull before the L70 could respond.

The blazing airship fell to the sea below, killing all of the crew and signalling the final death knell for the wider Naval Airship Division. Strasser's body was later recovered from the sea, showing no visible signs of injury or burning; his death may have been the result of a heart attack brought on by the airship's fatal descent. He was buried at sea and long-remembered as a flamboyant and passionate military commander.

Among the many tributes paid to him was a telling message from the Commander in Chief of the German High Seas Fleet, Vice-Admiral Reinhardt Scheer, who said,

> The airship, which was created by the inventive genius and stubborn perseverance of Count Zeppelin, was developed by Captain Peter Strasser, as Leader of Airships, with untiring zeal, and in spite of every obstacle, into a formidable weapon of attack. The spirit with which he succeeded in inspiring his particular arm on many an air raid he has crowned by his heroic death over England. As Count Zeppelin will live for ever in the grateful memory of the German people, so also will Captain Strasser, who led our airships to victory.

In 1931 Senior Lieutenant Horst Freiherr Treusch von Buttlar-Brandenfels, another of that select band of renowned airship commanders, published an account of some of the exploits of the Naval Airship Division in his highly entertaining book, *Zeppelins Over England*. In its preface is a heartfelt, and more accurate, homage to Peter Strasser from Vice-Admiral Adolf von Trotha:

> The men who in the dead of night and in all weathers, through a hail of incendiary shells and the inferno of anti-aircraft fire, bravely navigated our airships across the seas, serving with exemplary devotion and conscientiousness, and sacrificing their lives for the freedom of their country, had all been trained by him; the crews were inspired by his will, his spirit, and his enthusiasm, until he lost his life in the last naval airship attack on England. The only possible end to Peter Strasser's life was a hero's death, before the performance of duty and everything which he held most dear came to an end.

The 'Zeppelin field' in Theberton as it is today.

Ninety years after the crash the Zeppelin field in Theberton was again besieged by technicians, treasure-seekers and media cameras. This time the onslaught was more benign. During the summer of 2007 a survey carried out by the Great War Archaeological Group and filmed for the BBC's *Timewatch* series unearthed a number of artefacts, including wiring and girders from the wreckage and some fire-damaged buttons from a crewman's uniform. The dig involved aeronautical archaeologists, metal detectorists and aviation historians, and was the first excavation of a Zeppelin crash site in Britain. Having completed three years' research into the events surrounding the crash of the Zeppelin, this author was also invited to visit the archaeological site and provided the BBC with information about the final raid of the L48.

'The First Blitz' was subsequently screened by the BBC on Friday, 2 February 2007 and told the story of the first air campaign directed against Britain in the First World War. It highlighted the significant role played by German airships and the importance of the defensive measures put in place to combat this new form of aerial assault. That the excavation of the Zeppelin field produced only a limited sample of archaeological findings was testament to the thoroughness of the original navy technicians who painstakingly dissected every fragment of the L48 in the weeks following the crash. The knowledge gained from their work contributed to the airship development programme which flourished in Britain after the war and led to the construction of dirigibles like the R101 – an airship which would itself meet with disaster when it crashed into the north-west ridge of the Bois de Coutumes, near Beauvais, in northern France, during its maiden voyage to India. The ignition of its flammable hydrogen gas killed all but six of the fifty-four people on board.

Theberton itself remains a small, close-knit community of no more than 400 inhabitants. It sits inland from the Suffolk coast, close to the internationally renowned RSPB nature reserve at Minsmere. Walking in the early dawn of a warm summer morning on the outskirts of the village, it is hard now to imagine the drama and devastation that surrounded the flights and attacks of those early German airships, or to understand the alarm and panic of local people, as they became unwilling participants in a global conflict that killed and injured combatants and non-combatants alike, or to appreciate the emotions of a population that felt largely powerless under the onslaught of those early aerial weapons. It is harder still to walk through the ploughed field in which the L48 was finally laid to rest and envisage the terror of the airship crew as their lighter-than-air craft fell to earth in the breaking light of that warm June day.

Appendix A – Technical Glossary

Like all rigid airships, the L48 was essentially a powered balloon supported in its flight by a force equal to the weight of air it displaced, less the weight of the gas it carried in its numerous individual gas cells. The framework of the craft was equally straightforward in concept – rows of metal struts encasing the gas cells and covered in a weatherproof fabric. The whole airship was also streamlined to minimise wind resistance and facilitate the smooth passage of the aircraft through the air. Within, or attached to, this metal framework were all of the components required to support its powered flight: fuel tanks, engines, crew members, oil and water ballast.

The ascent of the Zeppelin required a lifting gas, one which would enable the aircraft to be lighter-than-air. In these early days of airship development the chosen gas was hydrogen, the lightest gas known. At standard temperature and pressure it is a colourless, odourless and tasteless gas and the most abundant of the chemical elements in the universe. It is also highly flammable and will burn violently in air. Pure hydrogen-oxygen flames burn in the ultra-violet colour range and are nearly invisible to the naked eye, making it difficult to detect visually if a hydrogen leak is burning. All of these factors made it a dangerous choice for use within a manned aircraft, as would be proven repeatedly during the First World War and beyond. In modern times the lifting gas of choice is helium, the second lightest gas known and a non-flammable element.

While the basic concepts surrounding the ability of the airship to fly may have been simple, there was nothing straightforward about the actual operation of the L48. Like any aircraft, it faced all of the usual challenges in taking to the air, from the need for lift, power and speed to the importance of steering, navigation, height and direction. Unlike an aeroplane, however, it also had to contend with the uncertainties of barometric pressure, humidity and temperature, in addition to the fluctuating weight of its lifting gas as the hydrogen became contaminated by air diffusing into the gas cells. The latter would have the effect of increasing the weight of the gas and thus decreasing the airship's lift.

Everything about the construction and flight of the airship was labour-intensive. It took months to build, using an army of specialist workers and component suppliers. In comparison with an aeroplane, it required a large crew and an even bigger complement of maintenance engineers back at base. Its take-off and landing depended on the many hundreds of operational ground crew employed at the Nordholz air base. Beyond the turbulent years of the war, the cost of running such a vast industry would be one of the most significant factors undermining the growth of commercial airship ventures.

As if all this were not enough to keep an anxious Zeppelin commander awake at night, the airship also had its military challenges to contend with. It defences were limited. The outer skin of the airship was covered in a black pigment to reduce its visibility to searchlights and its armaments consisted of a number of Maxim machine-guns in its gondolas. In addition, the L48's greatest defences lay in its stealth in flying at high altitude – beyond the range of anti-aircraft batteries and enemy aircraft – and the vigilance of its ever-wary crew members. In carrying out bombing raids, the L48 was also subject to the vagaries of its navigational and communications systems and the crudity of its bombing equipment. Little wonder then that the airship attacks on Britain throughout the whole of the war achieved little in the way of material damage. Where physical successes were recorded, many of them were more by luck than design.

What follows is a glossary of some of the key technical terms used throughout the book to assist the reader in understanding further how the L48 operated and differed from other aircraft:

Aerostat – a generic term for any lighter-than-air craft, which is not necessarily navigable, including balloons.

Airship – a generic term for any dirigible or powered lighter-than-air vehicle, including blimps and Zeppelins. Until the 1930s the word was used to refer to both lighter-than-air and heavier-than-air craft, but is now used only in relation to lighter-than-air craft.

Airspeed Meter – a device for measuring the speed through air in metres per second. Adjustments had to be made to its readings to take account of the decreased air density with increased altitude.

Altimeter – a barometer measuring air pressure, graduated to show the altitude in metres. False readings could be produced as a result of the barometric pressure after take-off.

Anoxia – the absence or reduced supply of oxygen in the atmosphere leading to a shortage of oxygen in the bloodstream and tissues of the body, creating hypoxia, or altitude sickness. In combination with this, the crews suffered as a result of the biting cold – the temperatures at altitude stiffening their joints, causing numbness, and occasionally resulting in frostbite. In response, the airshipmen took to wearing ever thicker layers of clothing.

Anti-freeze – the alcohol used in the engine cooling system and water ballast sacks.

Ballast – the weight carried aboard the airship to offset the buoyancy of its lifting gas or jettisoned to enable the craft to ascend more quickly. Most of the ballast in the L48 was carried along the keel in rubberised cloth sacks holding 2,200lbs of water. The water was released by levers in the control car.

Balloon – an unpowered lighter-than-air vehicle. These can be free – untethered and free to drift with the wind – or tethered to the ground (sometimes called kite balloons).

Blimp – a term coined in 1915 and used as a nickname for all small, non-rigid airships.

Bomb – the explosive bombs carried by the L48 were thick-walled and pear-shaped and came in different weights. Incendiary bombs were made of thermite wrapped in tarred rope. All bombs were carried in racks running along the keel and were released using a switchboard in the control car.

Bomb-sight – an instrument housed in the control car which was used by the executive officer and relied on settings for the ship's altitude and speed over the ground. While capable of some precision, its accurate use required skill and training.

Bow – the front end of the airship's hull.

Bracing wires – the struts used to hold parts of the airship's structure together.

Buoyancy – the ability of the airship to float by displacing a gas greater than its own weight. Buoyancy was controlled by the use of ballast.

Compass – a liquid magnetic direction finder which was carried in the control car close to the rudder man. Even with the addition of alcohol to the liquid within the instrument, the compass frequently froze at altitude.

Control car – the foremost car or gondola attached to the underneath of the airship. It was fully enclosed, with good all-round visibility. This was the flight station of the commander, executive officer, navigating officer, elevator man and rudder man. In the rear of the car was the sound-proofed radio cabin.

Crew – German naval airships carried a standard complement of crew members. For the L48 this consisted of eighteen naval officers. On its final raid the L48 was also carrying Corvette Captain Viktor Schütze, the overall Commander of the Naval Airship Division, who was acting as the senior airship officer coordinating the raid. Alongside Captain Schütze and Commander Franz Eichler, the crew was as follows:

Heinrich Ahrens – stoker petty officer
Wilhelm Betz – petty officer
Walter Dippmann – senior signalling officer
Heinrich Ellerkamm – machinist's mate
Wilhelm Gluckel – stoker petty officer
Paul Hannemann – boatwain's mate
Heinrich Herbst – signalman
Franz Konig – boatwain's mate
Wilhelm Meier – wireless operator
Otto Mieth – executive officer
Karl Milich – stoker petty officer
Michael Neunzig – stoker petty officer
Karl Ploger – senior sailor
Paul Suchlich – senior sailor
Wilhelm Uecker – machinist's mate
Hermann von Stockum – stoker petty officer
Paul Westphal – helmsman/navigator

Dead reckoning – the process of calculating the airship's position on the basis of the distance travelled on various headings since the last precisely observed or communicated position. Allowance had to be made for wind, air currents and compass errors. A series of ground stations enabled German airships to radio in for bearings and the triangulation of these enabled a precise position to be mapped during operations.

DELAG – the commercial airship company formed by Count Zeppelin in 1909, known as the *Deutsche Luftahrt Aktien-Gessellschaft.*

Dirigible – any steerable airship, including blimps, semi-rigid airships and Zeppelins (rigid airships). The term is a synonym for 'airship'.

Dope – the solution of cellulose acetate in acetone, which was mixed with black pigment and painted over the outer envelope of the airship. This tautened and waterproofed the aircraft and provided it with a degree of invisibility against searchlights.

Duraluminium – a lightweight but strong alloy of aluminium mixed with smaller amounts of copper, magnesium, manganese, iron and silicon. Its high strength-to-weight ratio made it the preferred choice for the main structure of rigid airships. Alfred Wilm patented the formula for the 'Duralumin' alloy in 1909 and granted an exclusive licence for its manufacture to the company Dürener Metallwerke.

Dynamic Lift – the vertical movement of the airship which was created by the aerodynamic forces acting on the hull of the aircraft, as opposed to its static lift (generated by the buoyancy of lifting gas).

Elevator – the movable horizontal hinged flap at the tail end of the airship for raising or depressing the tail section and enabling the aircraft to ascend or descend.

Engine cars – the small streamlined gondolas attached to the main hull of the airship which housed the engines of the airship and the crew required to maintain them.

Envelope – the gas bag of a pressure or semi-rigid airship. Unlike a rigid airship gas cell, an envelope forms an external barrier to the elements and when pressurised serves an integral role in maintaining the airship's shape. It also has fittings for attaching the fins, control car and other structural components. The envelope is usually made of a high-strength fabric combined with a sufficiently impermeable barrier coating or film to minimise loss of the buoyant gas it contains. Formerly made of rubberised cotton, envelopes are now constructed mainly of synthetic materials with their seams cemented, glued or sealed.

Gangway – the main route through the airship for the crew along the keel.

Gas cells – the gas-tight, balloon-like containers of lifting gas housed within the rigid framework of the airship. They were held in place by wire and cord netting and were designed to be as light as possible. Despite their gas-tight designs, gas loss was a consistent problem in Zeppelin airships.

Gas plant – the building where the hydrogen lifting gas was produced for filling airships.

Gondola – the term used to describe the variously shaped external pods on an airship that house engines or control rooms. The earliest airships had open-top, boat-shaped structures holding engines and crew. Later these structures were enclosed, giving rise to the terms 'control car' and 'engine car'.

Gravity tanks – the fuel tanks above the airship's engines which fed petrol by gravity. It was the job of the machinist's mate to keep these tanks filled by hand-pumping petrol up from the slip tanks in the keel.

Hangar – a large shed used to house an aircraft; the name is derived from the practice of deflating early airships when not in use and suspending them by straps from the roof of the building.

Height ceiling – the maximum altitude that an airship can reach under certain conditions. This would be affected by the useful load, barometric pressure and prevailing temperature.

Height-climber – the label given by the British to the new breed of Zeppelins produced from the early part of 1917 which were capable of flying at altitudes of between 16,000ft and 20,000ft – well above the anti-aircraft guns of the home defences and the fighter planes of the RFC. The L48 was one of this new breed of craft championed by Peter Strasser, the Leader of Airships in the German Naval Airship Division.

Hydrogen – the preferred lifting gas of Zeppelin airships. It was cheaply manufactured by a variety of methods, although the principal production process used on German airship bases was the Messerschmitt Process of passing steam over hot iron.

Keel – the triangular corridor running along the airship from end to end. At the bottom of the keel was the catwalk which was about 1ft wide and contained no handrails. Various items of equipment were slung from the box-girders along the keel.

Kite balloon – a captive balloon with a cylindrical envelope kept rigid and balanced to fly headlong into the wind. It was used for observation and defence purposes.

Lift – see 'Dynamic lift' and 'Static lift'.

Lighter-than-air – the branch of aeronautics or aerostatics that includes flying vehicles which depend on buoyancy from the displacement of air for their lift. This includes balloons and dirigibles of all types, whether piloted or not. In contrast, heavier-than-air craft are those which require air to pass over an aerofoil, such as a wing, to generate dynamic lift. This includes aeroplanes, gliders, helicopters and kites (whether piloted or not).

Maybach – an engine developed by Carl Maybach specifically for airships. The Maybach Motor Company was a Zeppelin subsidiary.

Maxim – the 8mm machine-guns that were standard issue on German naval airships throughout the war.

Mooring mast – a structure to which an airship is moored when not in flight.

Non-rigid airship – an airship in which the shape of the envelope is preserved by the pressure of air and the gas it contains, rather than by an internal framework. Airships of this type are sometimes referred to as 'pressure airships'.

Parachute – for a short time in early 1916 German naval airship crews had access to individual 'attached' parachutes, but these were soon abandoned because of their impact on the overall weight of the airship.

Powered dynamic lift – the positive or negative force on the airship's hull derived from driving it at an angle with the power of the aircraft's engines. At full power and at an angle of around 8 degrees, an airship could develop a dynamic lift of several tons.

Propeller – the propellers of the L48 were two-bladed and constructed by the German Garuda company from laminations of West African and Honduras mahogany and European or American walnut. These were geared down to 540rpm from an engine speed of around 1,400rpm and were 17ft in diameter.

Rigid airship – an airship whose shape is maintained by an internal framework and whose lifting gas is contained in separate gas cells within that structure. The external envelope on a rigid airship is not completely gas-tight, but does protect the more delicate gas cells and other interior components from wind and weather and provides streamlining. Rigid airships included Zeppelins and similar aircraft built by other companies.

Rudder – a vertical flap, hinged in such a way as to allow the motion of the airship to be steered from port to starboard. It was located at the tail of the L48.

Schütte-Lanz – a rigid airship manufacturing company founded in Mannheim-Rheinau, Germany, by Johann Schütte and Karl Lanz. From 1909 it was a competitor to the Zeppelin Company and introduced a number of innovative refinements to airship design. Their airships were generally more streamlined, although their plywood girders (favoured over the metal structures of Zeppelins) were weakened by exposure to moisture.

Slip tanks – the main fuel tanks of the airship located along the keel. Petrol was hand-pumped from these into gravity tanks above the motors in each engine car.

Static lift – the vertical force exerted on an airship which is created solely by the buoyancy of its lifting gas (in contrast to its dynamic lift).

Streamlining – the smooth, aerodynamically efficient shape of an airship designed to produce minimal wind resistance or 'drag'. Streamlining tests of Zeppelins were done at the Friedrichshafen plant.

Thermometer – the control car of the L48 contained an air thermometer and an electronic thermometer which could remotely read the temperature in one of the internal gas cells. Both instruments were essential in determining the lift of the airship and the impact of 'superheating' (due to the sun's heat) or 'supercooling' (the drop in gas temperature experienced at night).

Trim – the balance of the airship in the air in response to static forces. With weights and lifting forces properly balanced around the centre of gravity, the airship would be in trim, otherwise known as being on an 'even keel'.

Trolley – a wheeled truck that was pulled by hand along docking rails, to which ropes from the airship could be attached for take-off and landing purposes.

Useful lift – the lift generated by the airship after subtracting the weight of the aircraft itself and its hydrogen lifting gas. This would determine the 'useful load', or the amount of equipment and supplies that could then be carried (fuel, ballast, crew, armaments, etc.).

Valving-off – the process of admitting or shutting off gases in the gas cells to prevent overpressure and to level out the differences in air pressure between the lifting gas and the surrounding atmosphere.

Weighing-off – the process of adjusting the precise weight of the craft so that it is able to float in trim. This could be achieved by releasing ballast (if the airship was sinking in the air) or valving-off gas (if the airship was rising in the air).

Zeppelin – often used as a generic term for any rigid airship, although it is derived from the name of its inventor and promoter, Ferdinand Graf von Zeppelin. The first aircraft of this type flew in 1900 near Friedrichshafen, Germany. After many trials and tribulations, Zeppelin was able to form a company, Luftschiffbau-Zeppelin, to manufacture this type of rigid airship.

Appendix B – A Chronology of Airship History in East Anglia, 1914–45

1914

The War Office announces that the newly established Royal Naval Air Service (RNAS) is to become responsible for Britain's small fleet of non-rigid airships. At the outbreak of war in August 1914 the number of operational airships stands at seven. In response to the threat of German U-boat attacks, the Admiralty decides with some haste to commission the construction of a fleet of new airships for aerial patrols over the North Sea. A Coastal Airship Station at Pulham in Norfolk is to open a year and a half later as a base for such patrols, amid an on-going aerial bombing campaign by Germany – the first of its kind in Britain.

1915

19 January – Great Yarmouth becomes the first English town to be bombed from the air. Naval Zeppelin L3, commanded by Hans Fritz, drops eight 110lb high explosive bombs on the undefended town, killing a 50-year-old man and a 72-year-old widow and destroying a number of properties. The airship L4 carries out a similar attack on King's Lynn, killing a 26-year-old war widow and a boy of 14 and injuring thirteen others, before heading out across The Wash. During the raid other bombs are dropped on Beeston, Sheringham, Brancaster, Heacham, Snettisham, Dersingham and Grimston.

13 April – the Zeppelin airships L5, L6 and L7 set off to bomb targets on the River Humber but end up over East Anglia instead. L5 bombs Henham and Lowestoft, destroying a number of buildings and setting fire to a timber yard. The L7 crosses the Norfolk coast the same night but fails to drop any bombs.

29 April – Zeppelin raiders make a series of attacks on English targets, including the Suffolk town of Bury St Edmunds.

9 August – Zeppelin L11 drops its bombs in the sea off Lowestoft, its captain wrongly concluding that the airship is over the port of Harwich.

12 August – four Zeppelin airships attempt to attack England. Encountering poor weather, only two are able to reach any targets – the L10 bombing Woodbridge, Ipswich and Harwich.

13 September – three German airships take off to raid London. The L13 is met with heavy anti-aircraft fire over Harwich and fails to reach its target. It is hit by one of twelve rounds fired by anti-aircraft guns at Felixstowe.

5 October – five Zeppelin raiders are dispatched to attack London. The L11 comes inland along the East Anglian coast, where it comes under fire from the coastal defences, before jettisoning bombs on the Norfolk villages of Horstead, Coltishall and Great Hautbois. The L16 drops bombs on the town of Hertford.

13 October – Zeppelin L11 bombs villages in South Norfolk.

1916
31 January – nine Zeppelin raiders take off for England, with Peter Strasser, the Leader of Airships, coordinating the attack aboard the L11. The L16 drops bombs on what its captain believes to be Great Yarmouth. In fact these fall into the sea between the town and nearby Lowestoft. Two high explosive bombs do fall on Swaffham in Norfolk, however. Encountering engine trouble, the L17 drifts over the Norfolk coast near Sheringham before dropping its bombs in fields close to Holt. The L19 comes down in the North Sea on its

return journey, the crew being forced to cling to the wreckage of the airship.

1 February – the floating wreck of the L19 is spotted by a British steam-trawler, the *King Stephen*. The captain speaks to the Zeppelin crew, but refuses to rescue them, claiming later that he feared they might overpower his crew and take over the ship. By the time the *King Stephen* reaches port, the airship has sunk and all of the crew have drowned. A number of the airshipmen write final messages, which they seal in bottles and throw into the sea. One from Commander Loewe, addressed to Peter Strasser, reads:

> With fifteen men on the upper platform, roof, and body of L19 (minus cars), drifting at about longitude 3 degrees east, I am trying to write a final report. What with three engine breakdowns and light head-wind on the homeward flight my return was delayed, and I got into a fog over Holland, where we met with heavy rifle fire. Ship became very heavy, and three of our engines broke down simultaneously. February the 2nd, 1916, at about 1 pm, probably our last hour.

A second message from Loewe reads: 'We have been drifting about two days and two nights. No help! Best wishes! An English steam-trawler has refused to rescue us.' A separate message from one of the crew names the *King Stephen*, from Grimsby, as the trawler in question. When news of the incident becomes known, there is widespread anger among German naval officers.

February – the Pulham Air Station, or no. 2 Coastal Airship Station, is commissioned, the site having been purchased by the Admiralty in 1915. After a colourful operational history spanning nearly fifty years, the 762-acre site is finally sold by the Air Ministry on 20 July 1962 for just over £57,000.

31 March – Zeppelin raiders drop bombs in the Stowmarket area of Suffolk. An anti-aircraft battery manages to damage the L13, forcing it to return to base.

24 April – eight Zeppelin raiders are given the order to 'attack south England, London if at all possible'. The airships approach England along the Norfolk coast and drop bombs close to Newmarket in Suffolk. One of the airships drops forty-five bombs on the village of Dilham in Norfolk, during which a woman dies of fright.

25 April – Great Yarmouth is bombarded during a naval raid by the German High Seas Fleet. Among the vessels torpedoed that night is the armed steam-trawler *King Stephen*, which had earlier failed to rescue the downed crew of Zeppelin L19 on the night of 1 February. The ship's crew are rescued and taken prisoner, all of the men denying emphatically that they had been on the *King Stephen* during the earlier encounter with the Zeppelin crew.

31 August – the first coastal airship is received by the Pulham Air Station. The base begins to carry out patrols over the southern North Sea and its airships are nicknamed the 'Pulham Pigs'.

September – the Shorts Brothers Engineering Company decides to create a new construction facility for the British airships it has been contracted to build. A site in Cardington, Bedfordshire, is chosen for the construction, later to become the Royal Airship Works and the home of the ill-fated airship R101.

2 September – the largest Zeppelin raid of the war is carried out, involving sixteen German airships. The wooden-framed Schütte-Lanz airship SL11 is shot down over Cuffley, Hertfordshire, by Lieutenant William Leefe Robinson, of the RFC's home defence squadron at Hornchurch, Essex. All crew members are lost. It is the first German airship to be brought down over British soil and earns Robinson the Victoria Cross. Other airships in the raiding party manage to drop bombs on Norfolk and Suffolk.

23 September – a raiding party of twelve German airships sets out to attack London. Zeppelin L33 crash-lands near

Little Wigborough, Essex, after coming under attack from RFC fighters and its crew is taken prisoner. The L32 is shot down near Billericay, Essex, by Lieutenant Frederick Sowrey in a BE2c aircraft. All crew members are lost.

2 October – Zeppelin L31 is shot down over Potters Bar, Hertfordshire, by Lieutenant Wulstan Tempest of the RFC's home defence squadron based at North Weald Bassett. All crew members are lost.

27 November – another Zeppelin raiding party brings heavy losses to the German fleet command. L34 is shot down over the North Sea, while the L21 is brought down to the west of Lowestoft by three RNAS pilots flying out of Burgh Castle, Norfolk, and Bacton, Suffolk. All crew members are lost.

1917
13 February – Colonel Maitland, the first man to parachute from a British airship, makes a successful parachute drop from the British airship C17 while it is flying at 1,000ft above the Pulham Air Station.

April – Pulham-based airship C17 is shot down over the southern North Sea by German seaplanes. All crew members are lost.

8 April – British airship NS1 arrives at Pulham Air Station for scouting missions. This was the last non-rigid airship to be developed during the First World War.

14 April – an explosion of the silicol gas plants at the Pulham Air Station kills two men.

23 May – six German airships cross the North Sea to attack London. The Leader of Airships Peter Strasser joins the crew of the L44. In addition to some strikes close to the capital, bombs are dropped near Mildenhall, East Dereham, East Wrentham and Great Ryburgh. The L40 and L45 claim also to have bombed Norwich, although evidence of their bombing raids is scarce. After suffering a number of debilitating engine failures, the L44 hovers above Harwich before being forced to return to its base.

14 June – Zeppelin L43 is shot down over the North Sea by a Felixstowe-based H12 Curtiss Flying Boat piloted by Flight Sub-Lieutenant B.D. Hobbs. All of its twenty-four crew members are lost.

16/17 June – six German airships are dispatched to attack southern England. Only the L42 and L48 complete the sea crossing. The L42 successfully bombs Ramsgate. The L48 is shot down over the Suffolk coast and crashes at Theberton. Three members of the crew survive – the first and last Zeppelin crew members to survive the crash of a burning airship over England.

27 June – British airship NS2 crashes near Stoneham, on the outskirts of Stowmarket, on a trial flight from Kingsnorth to Pulham.

19 October – eleven German airships leave bases in Nordholz, Tondern, Ahlhorn and Wittmundhaven for attacks on central England. The L54 drops bombs in open country between Ipswich and Colchester, believing that the airship is over Derby and Nottingham. It is nearly shot down by a BE2c fighter plane from Great Yarmouth. The L46 attempts an attack on Norwich, but its twenty bombs fall instead on Happisburgh in North Norfolk. The L47 drops bombs to the west of Ipswich in Suffolk, its captain believing the airship to be close to Nottingham. The L53 manages to drop bombs on a military school and engineering works in Bedford, while the L49 drops forty-two bombs across Norfolk, to the west of Norwich, to little effect.

11 December – Pulham-based airship C27 is shot down by German seaplanes while on a coastal patrol over the North Sea. All crew members are lost.

12 December – Pulham-based airship C26 is brought down at Eesmess in Holland having run out of fuel. All of the crew are captured and held as prisoners of war.

1918
12 April – Zeppelin L62 drops bombs in the open countryside of Norfolk en route to its operational targets in the industrial Midlands.

5 August – the last German airship raid of the war is carried out involving Zeppelins L53, L56, L63, L65 and L70. The L70 is shot down off the coast of East Anglia by Majors Egbert Cadbury and Robert Leckie in a Yarmouth-based DH4. On board the airship is Peter Strasser, the Leader of Airships. He is lost along with the rest of the crew.

28 October – the Italian airship SR1 leaves Ciampino to fly across France and on to its new permanent base at the Pulham Air Station. The craft arrives on 6 November having encountered a number of operational problems. Each member of the crew is decorated after the flight, the Italian Government awarding the Croix de Guerre to Captain Meager, while Captain Williams receives the Air Force Cross.

6 November – the R31, the first airship to be constructed in Shed 1 of the Cardington Royal Airship Works, is commissioned exactly two years and two months from the date on which construction first started. The armistice of the First World War takes place five days later.

1919
9 February – Pulham-based airship R26 is damaged while moored in snowy conditions. The damage is so severe that the airship is scrapped later that month.

March – British airship R33 arrives at Pulham Air Station to start operational duties. Between 18 June 1919 and 14 October 1920 the airship makes twenty-three flights and is airborne for 337 hours.

13 July – British airship R34 arrives at Pulham Air Station following a successful 3,130 mile double-crossing of the North Atlantic.

23 July – British airship NS11 encounters difficulties while flying in thundery conditions from Pulham to Kingsnorth. The craft is struck by lightning over Cley, Norfolk, and crashes in flames. All crew members are lost.

9 August – Sergeant Lee carries out a parachute trial at Pulham, jumping from the airship SR1 while it is flying at 2,000ft. His descent takes nearly four-and-a-half minutes.

6 September – British airship R32 arrives at Pulham Air Station for operational duties.

1920
22 June – the first of two Zeppelins which were handed over to the British Government as war reparations arrives at Pulham Air Station. The L64 is flown by its former crew.

30 June – Zeppelin L71 is flown from northern Germany to its new home at Pulham Air Station to join the L64.

20 September – the Air Ministry orders that all construction work on British airships should cease, although work on the R38 at Cardington is allowed to continue. The airship is later sold to the Americans for £500,000.

1921
February – the formal order is given for work to cease on the construction of the R37, the second airship to be built in Shed 1 of the Cardington Royal Airship Works. Some 90 per cent of the work on the craft is complete and the airship is left to stand in the shed alongside the completed R38. All of the construction workers are laid off and the airship is later dismantled.

2 April – British airship R36 arrives at Pulham Air Station for operational duties. It is based on designs derived originally from Zeppelin L48. Its construction had begun before the end of the First World War.

May – the R38 is flown from Cardington to the Howden Airship Station in Yorkshire.

21 June – the R36 is badly damaged while returning to Pulham from a local flight. Although repairs are made, the airship never flies again.

20 August – British airship R80 arrives at Pulham air base for operational duties.

24 August – British airship R38 breaks up and catches fire over the River Humber en route to Pulham. All but five of the forty-nine people on board are killed. Among the dead is Air Commodore Maitland, the 'father of British airships', and a commanding officer of the Pulham Air Station.

1924
1 November – a contract is signed for the construction of the R101 at the decommissioned Cardington Royal Airship Works. The airship is planned to be one of two dirigibles forming a new Imperial Airship Service between the United Kingdom and India.

1925
2 April – the R33 is removed from Shed 1 of the newly recommissioned Cardington Royal Airship Works to be reconditioned for service. It has lain in its berth for more than four years since the closure of the base after the First World War. Within days it is flown to the Pulham Air Station.

17 April – the R33 survives a potentially disastrous flight over the North Sea having been dislodged from its mooring mast at the Pulham Air Station in high winds the previous day.

5 October – the repaired R33 is brought out from its shed at the Pulham Air Station to begin pressure experiments linked

to the construction of the R101 at the Cardington Royal
Airship Works.

1926

11 April – the semi-rigid airship *Norge* arrives at the Pulham
Air Station flown by the celebrated Italian airship
commander General Umberto Nobile. The airship is en route
to the Arctic from Italy carrying Norwegian explorer Roald
Amundsen, who is hoping to be the first to reach the North
Pole by air, having failed in two previous attempts by flying
boat.

13 April – Umberto Nobile's *Norge* leaves the Pulham Air
Station for Oslo on the next stop of its Arctic adventure.
While the airship is later to make the first successful aerial
crossing of the North Pole, Roald Amundsen is actually
beaten to the polar icecap by two American airmen in the
Josephine Ford, a Fokker airplane. They are the first to look
down on the North Pole, having flown a circular route from
King's Bay near Spitsbergen in Norway. Later, in the summer
of 1928, Amundsen is to die in a second aerial crossing
attempt.

1930

5 October – the British airship R101 crashes into the north-
west ridge of the Bois de Coutumes near Beauvais in northern
France during its maiden voyage to India. Only six of the fifty-
four on board survive the fire that consumes the airship. A
number of those on board have East Anglian connections and
much of the design and primary structure of the airship was
the work of Norfolk firm Boulton & Paul.

1936

November – the Cardington Royal Airship Works becomes an
RAF station and takes on responsibility for the development
and creation of thousands of kite balloons in the Second World
War. It is to be used to train balloon operators and drivers and
at its peak produces twenty-six balloons a week.

1939

August – the newly commissioned German airship *Graf Zeppelin* carries out spying missions off the East Anglian coast prior to the outbreak of hostilities in the Second World War.

1941

16 February – Pulham Air Station comes under attack from a Luftwaffe bomber which releases its bomb-load on to an old airship shed at the base. Only minimal damage is sustained.

Appendix C – A Chronology of Zeppelin Airships After 1918

ount Zeppelin died of pneumonia in Berlin on 8 March 1917 at the age of 78. The company he had set up continued under the leadership of managing director Alfred Colsman. Despite the armistice, the company began design work on a new class of small civilian airships for short-range services.

With the retirement of Colsman and the provisions of the Treaty of Versailles, the Zeppelin Company looked doomed. Under the terms of the Versailles Treaty, the company was ordered to cease airship construction and surrender its two newly constructed commercial Zeppelins (*Nordstern* and *Bodensee*) as part of Germany's war reparations. The company was also forbidden to build any further military craft or any commercial airships with a capacity of more than a million cubic feet (the minimum capacity required by an airship to cross the Atlantic).

In 1922, after a period of considerable commercial turmoil, the Zeppelin Company was taken over by Dr Hugo Eckener, who later became its chairman. Under his stewardship the organisation built good relations with the USA and eventually struck deals for the construction of a new breed of giant airships.

1919

23 June – a week before the Treaty of Versailles is signed, Zeppelins L41, L42, L52, L56, L63 and L65 are destroyed by their former crews at the Nordholz airship base to prevent them being taken into enemy hands. The action follows the scuttling of surrendered German warships by their crews at Scapa Flow only two days before.

20 August – the Zeppelin *Bodensee* enters commercial service. In the next ninety-eight days it is to make over a hundred flights between Friedrichshafen and Berlin, carrying nearly 2,500 passengers. It is later to be handed over to Italy as part of Germany's war reparations, in part-compensation for the destruction of the six airships on 23 June. Renamed *Esperia*, it is finally broken up in July 1928.

1920

28 August – Zeppelins L30 and L37 are dismantled according to the terms of the Treaty of Versailles and their separate parts are sent to Belgium and Japan respectively. Both nations have no suitable hangars for the craft, but retain important airship parts. Zeppelin L61 is handed over to Italy as part of Germany's war reparations.

1921

13 June – the airship *Nordstern* is handed over to France as part of Germany's war reparations. It is renamed *Méditerranée* and remains in service until 1927.

16 December – a conference of ambassadors from various nations approves the request of the United States Government to have an airship similar to Zeppelin L70 built at Friedrichshafen for delivery to the USA. This is later to become Zeppelin LZ126.

1923

4 September – Zeppelin L49, which was forced down in France during October 1917 and captured intact before being handed over to the USA, is relaunched for the first time under its new name USS *Shenandoah* (a Native American word meaning 'daughter of the stars'). The 680ft airship is the first to use inert helium as its lifting gas.

21 December – having been handed over to France as part of Germany's war reparations and renamed *Dixmude*, Zeppelin L72 crashes in an explosion off Sciacca, near Sicily, while returning from a flight over Africa. All of its crew of fifty-two are lost.

1924
12 October – Zeppelin LZ126, built at Friedrichshafen, takes off for a flight across the Atlantic. It is handed over to the USA and is renamed USS *Los Angeles*.

1925
3 September – the American-owned airship USS *Shenandoah* (previously Zeppelin L49) breaks up in a storm over Ohio, killing nineteen of its forty-three crew members. The airship had completed fifty-six flights, covering over 25,000 miles.

1 December – the Locarno Treaty is signed lifting all Allied restrictions on the building of airships in Germany.

1928
8 July – the newly constructed airship *Graf Zeppelin* is christened by the daughter of Count Zeppelin, Countess Brandenstein-Zeppelin. The building of the airship was the result of fund-raising by Dr Hugo Eckener and Dr Ludwig Dürr (the chief designer of the L48) and took advantage of the Locarno Treaty of 1925.

18 September – the *Graf Zeppelin* flies for the first time. With a length of 776ft and a gas capacity of 2,650,000ft^3, the craft is the largest airship ever constructed. Its flight lasts for over three hours and is so successful that a long-range test flight is scheduled for the next day.

11 October – the *Graf Zeppelin* departs for its first commercial passenger air service across the North Atlantic. The flight takes passengers down the valley of the River Rhone, across the Mediterranean, over Madeira and the Azores and over the Atlantic to the eastern seaboard of the USA. Having passed over Washington, Baltimore, Philadelphia and New York, the airship finally arrives at Lakehurst on 15 October, having been airborne for nearly 112 hours.

29 October – the *Graf Zeppelin* makes the 4,560-mile return journey back across the Atlantic, reaching Friedrichshafen after almost 72 hours in the air.

1929
24 March – having embarked on a series of short flights, the *Graf Zeppelin* departs on a trip to the Middle East covering 4,790 miles.

15 August – the *Graf Zeppelin* leaves Friedrichshafen for an historic 'round the world' flight. In addition to the crew, it is carrying eighteen paying passengers, two journalists and 1,100lb of mail and freight. Among its many adventures, the airship encounters a typhoon as it is approaching Japan. During its six flight stages the Zeppelin flies some 21,250 miles without any major delays or technical problems. It arrives back at the Friedrichshafen base on 4 September.

1931
4 April – the American airship USS *Akron*, which was built using Zeppelin patents, is lost in a storm over the Atlantic. All but three of its crew of seventy-six are drowned.

24 July – the *Graf Zeppelin* begins a flight of exploration over the North Pole, collecting scientific data on the magnetic field, temperature, air pressure and humidity of the polar icecap.

1935
12 February – the American airship USS *Macon*, which, like its sister-ship the USS *Akron*, was built using Zeppelin patents, is lost during routine operations off the coast of southern California. Two men drown, but the remaining eighty-one crew members are rescued.

1936
4 March – the first trial flight of the newly constructed airship *Hindenburg*. The 804ft airship is named after Paul von Hindenburg, the former President of Germany (1847–1934).

22 March – the *Hindenburg* and *Graf Zeppelin* take off for propaganda flights in support of the election of Adolf Hitler for a second term as Germany's Chancellor. They remain in the air for four days, dropping pro-Hitler leaflets and broadcasting military music.

31 March – the *Hindenburg* begins its first commercial flight from southern Germany to Santa Cruz, near Rio de Janeiro, covering 13,500 miles.

1937
6 May – in its second year of service, having flown sixty-three times, the *Hindenburg* is destroyed by a fire while landing at Lakehurst Naval Air Station in Manchester, New Jersey, USA. Thirty-six people (one-third of those on board) perish in the accident, which is widely reported by film, photographic and radio media. As a result of the crash, its sister-ship the *Graf Zeppelin* is grounded, having completed 590 flights over a distance of over a million miles, and carrying over 13,000 passengers. It ends its days as a museum exhibit in Frankfurt.

1938
14 September – the *Graf Zeppelin II* flies for the first time. Despite plans for commercial flights, the airship is taken over by the German authorities for experimental purposes, including reconnaissance flights along the coast of Britain in the period prior to the Second World War. The Zeppelin is later broken up for scrap in a Frankfurt hangar during March 1940. Although the Zeppelin Company makes no further airships, it stays in business assembling the long-range V2 rocket missiles launched at Britain during the final stages of the war. When this becomes known to the Allies the Friedrichshafen factory is bombed by British and American bombers, destroying all of the hangars and airship facilities on the site.

1945
The Allies order the liquidation of the Zeppelin Company.

1969
Dutch engineer Gerhard Hoffmann, who was employed by the Zeppelin Company as a route-planner in the 1930s, puts forward ideas for the construction of a small Zeppelin airship

modelled on the 1919 dirigible *Bodensee*. He creates the concept and plans for a new *Olympia Zeppelin* to be used during the 1972 Olympic Games. Combined with proposals for a new national airship programme, his ideas are presented to Gustav Heinemann, the President of the German Federal Republic, who asks the German Aerospace Society (or DGLR) to consider the proposals. Despite a considerable period of research and investigation, no airship results from the proposals.

1997
18 September – the maiden flight of the experimental airship *Friedrichshafen* takes place, the successor to the original Zeppelin Company having restarted airship construction in 1996. The airship is only one-third the size of its Zeppelin predecessors and is of a semi-rigid design known as Zeppelin NT (new technology). Regular tourist flights across Germany begin, the airship carrying twelve passengers and two crew members.

2004
June – a Zeppelin NT airship is sold for the first time to a Japanese company, the Nippon Airship Corporation, for tourism and advertising mainly around Tokyo.

2007
21 September – a Zeppelin NT airship, used by the De Beers mining company for an exploration project to locate potential diamond mines in the remote Kalahari Desert, is severely damaged by a whirlwind while in Botswana.

Acknowledgements and Select Bibliography

Zeppelin Over Suffolk is a piece of historical investigative journalism portraying real people and events. The research for the book was based on media accounts, personal records and other contemporary and historical sources. My principal aim was to produce an accurate and informative account of the remarkable events that occurred during the summer of 1917. Any errors or omissions in the story are my own.

Had it not been for a chance discussion with a relative, the book might never have seen the light of day. I am therefore extremely indebted to my good friend and brother-in-law Gary Sharman, who first inspired me to write the story of the L48 and relayed to me the folklore about the airship. My thanks must also go to my wife Jacqueline, who acted as a much appreciated and involuntary researcher, scouring many a library shelf and second-hand bookstore for relevant material on German airships. I could not have completed the book without her faith and support for my venture.

Of the many other people who helped me, I would also like to express my particular appreciation for the assistance provided by the staff and trustees of the Leiston Long Shop Museum. Frank Huxley gave me access to his collection of original crash site photographs which have been used throughout the book. Stephen and Julia Mael provided invaluable information and support. The museum itself has a wealth of material and artefacts about the final raid of the L48. John Waddell, a relative of the original crash site photographer J.S. Waddell, kindly provided me with access to a previously unpublished picture of the gravestones of the airship crew. My thanks go to them all.

I have set out below a select bibliography of the principal sources of printed information used in the compilation of the book for those who may wish to carry out their own research into the period or events portrayed. The newspapers and journals consulted included *The Times*, *Daily Mail*, *East Anglian Magazine*, *Eastern Daily Press*, *Evening Star* and *Daily Herald*, *Norwich Mercury*, *Leiston Observer*, *East Anglian Daily Times* and *Cross and Cockade*.

Botting, Douglas, *Dr Eckener's Dream Machine* (HarperCollins Publishers, 2001)

Briggs, Asa, *A Social History of England* (Weidenfeld & Nicholson, 1983)

Brooks, Peter, *Historic Airships* (Hugh Evelyn Ltd, 1973)

Brown, Malcolm, *The Imperial War Museum Book of the First World War* (Sidgwick & Jackson, 1991)

Buttlar-Brandenfels, Freiherr Treusch von, *Zeppelins over England* (George G. Harrap & Company Ltd, 1931)

Chamberlain, Geoffrey, *Airships – Cardington* (Terence Dalton Ltd, 1984)

Chant, Christopher, *Zeppelin, The History of German Airships from 1900 to 1937* (David & Charles, 2000)

Delve, Ken, *Nightfighter, The Battle for the Night Skies* (Arms & Armour Press, 1995)

Dymond, David and Northeast, Peter, *A History of Suffolk* (Phillimore & Co. Ltd, 1995)

Gilbert, Martin, *The First World War* (Weidenfeld & Nicholson, 1994)

Griehl, Manfred, and Dressel, Joachim, *Zeppelin! The German Airship Story* (Arms & Armour Press, 1990)

Kinsey, Gordon, *Pulham Pigs* (Terence Dalton Ltd, 1988)

Lehmann, Captain Ernst, and Mingos, Howard, *The Zeppelins: The Development of the Airship, with the Story of the Zeppelins' Air Raids in the World War* (Sears & Company Inc., 1927)

Marben, Rolf, *Zeppelin Adventures* (John Hamilton Ltd, 1931)

Mee, Arthur, *The King's England: Suffolk, Our Farthest East* (Hodder & Stoughton Ltd, 1947)

Nitske, Robert, *The Zeppelin Story* (AS Barnes & Company Inc., 1977)

Nowarra, Heinz, *German Airships, Parseval, Schütte, Lanz, Zeppelin* (Schiffer Publishing Ltd, 1991)

Phelps, Humphrey, *The Old Photographs Series, Walberswick to Felixstowe* (Chalford Publishing Company Ltd, 1994)

Porter, Valerie, *Yesterday's Countryside, Country Life as it Really Was* (David & Charles, 2000)

Robinson, Douglas, *The Zeppelin in Combat* (Schiffer Publishing Ltd, 1994)

Suffolk Federation of Women's Institutes, *Suffolk Within Living Memory* (Countryside Books, 1994)

Taylor, John, *A History of Aerial Warfare* (Hamlyn Publishing Group Ltd, 1974)

Toland, John, *Ships in the Sky* (Frederick Muller Ltd, 1957)

Treadwell, Terry, and Wood, Alan, *Airships of the First World War* (Tempus Publishing Ltd, 1999)

Waddell, J.S., *Pictorial Souvenir of the 'Strafed' Zeppelin L48* (The Hayling Studio (Leiston), 1917)

Wells, H.G., *The War in the Air* (Penguin Books Ltd, 1973)

Index